CUISINE
GRAND-MERE

CUISINE
GRAND-MERE

Traditional
French Home Cooking

MARIE-PIERRE MOINE

Ebury Press
London

Pour Mado — Madame Marcel Morange

First published in Great Britain in 1990
by Barrie & Jenkins Ltd

Revised edition published 2001

1 3 5 7 9 10 8 6 4 2

Text © Marie-Pierre Moine 1990, 2001
Illustrations © Retrograph Archive Collection

Ebury Press
Random House, 20 Vauxhall Bridge Road, London SW1V 2SA

Random House Australia (Pty) Limited
20 Alfred Street, Milsons Point, Sydney, New South Wales 2061, Australia

Random House New Zealand Limited
18 Poland Road, Glenfield, Auckland 10, New Zealand

Random House South Africa (Pty) Limited
Endulini, 5A Jubilee Road, Parktown 2193, South Africa

The Random House Group Limited Reg. No. 954009

www.randomhouse.co.uk

A CIP catalogue record for this book is available from the British Library.

Edited by Beverly LeBlanc
Designed by David Fordham
Picture research by Philippa Lewis and Jilliana Ranicar-Breese
Line drawings by Philip Hood

Printed in Portugal
Typeset by MATS, Southend-on-Sea, Essex

ISBN 0 09 187890 X

Contents

Introduction 7

A Few Remarks 12

Potages/*Soups* 16

Hors d'Œuvre/*Starters* 28

Entrées Chaudes/*Hot Starters* 40

Poissons et Fruits de Mer/*Fish and Seafood* 60

Volailles et Viandes/*Poultry, Game and Meat* 86

Légumes/*Vegetables* 120

Desserts/*Desserts* 136

Index 156

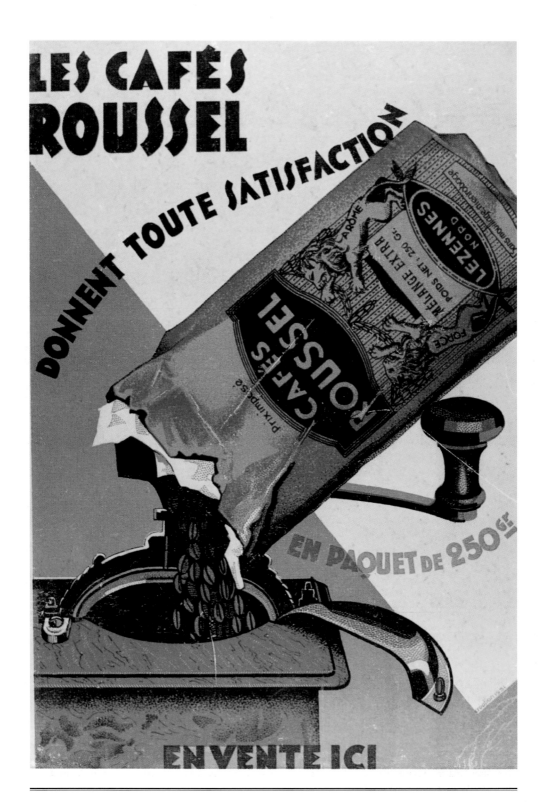

INTRODUCTION

SOME OF MY happiest childhood memories are of my grandparents' kitchen at Fourchettes, their house near Amboise in the Loire valley. This is troglodyte country, the land of cave dwellers, and the Fourchettes kitchen was, in fact, such a cave, separate from the house, carved out of the rocks sixty feet beneath the wood that led up to the edge of the vineyards. The cave-kitchen was a magic place. It was empty of cheerful Fifties' gadgets, but full of mysteries and large enough for us as small children to test our cycling skills around the old table when nobody was watching. It was cool in summer and mild in winter, with patches of green damp stubbornly coming up through the whitewash on the 'walls'.

I loved it for its strangeness and for the myriad good things that came from it. It was presided over by Madeleine, my grandmother's cook, who had been in the family much longer than I, and was my youngest aunt's godmother. She was the genius of the place, radiating good humour and energy. The grown-ups, after most meals, nodded their heads contentedly and commented without fail that she was 'vraiment une bonne cuisinière, une très, très, bonne cuisinière, une excellente cuisinière.' I didn't have a great deal to compare Mado to, but, yes, her food tasted better than the food I normally ate, certainly much better than that I had at my parents' in Paris.

Like all magic places, the kitchen had its dangers. The huge black range that Mado kept constantly burning daunted me, a tame volcano on one side of the cave. On the other side was an ancient refrigerator so badly earthed that we children weren't allowed near it. I once disobeyed the rule and tried to open its door to steal an illicit œuf à la neige. It was siesta time and I was barefoot:; the shock was so violent that my aunt, who tried to prize me off, got stuck to the refrigerator too. Fortunately, someone else made a dash for the fuse box and I live to tell the tale, wear sandals when raiding refrigerators, and still eat œufs à la neige.

The grass was greener on vacation, of course, but knowing that there was going to be a tarte à l'oignon or profiteroles for dinner added a glow to the afternoon. I always asked about the menu, helped pick for it in the garden, and reported faithfully to the kitchen most evenings after my bath, to tail beans and stir the vinaigrette, hoping to lick a few spoons here and there, while Madeleine, eyes watering from peeling onions, fed me family gossip, solved grievances and explained why evaporated milk was better than cream in onion tart . . . . Nor was I the only one listening, for the kitchen was the newsroom and general refuge of the family – Mado knew everything, wasn't partisan and dispensed sympathy, jokes common sense. She invariably had an audience around the oiled cloth of the central table while she hovered between the big kitchen range and the chipped enamel sink. More often than not, the adults present had a glass of 'Fourchettes' wine in hand, to be concealed at once if my grandfather happened to walk in. That distinguished gentleman's pride and joy, the pick of his vineyard, his better bottles, so temptingly labelled 'pour les grandes occasions' and more eminently drinkable than the ordinary wine he normally produced, had a habit of disappearing from his cave, the wine-cellar cave next door. His temper was formidable and we were terrified of it – very right, too: after all, it was his house. But the kitchen never really seemed to be under his jurisdiction.

Cuisine grand-mère is traditional French home cooking, the repertoire of dishes that are eaten en famille and as party pieces, recipes handed down from grandmother to mother to daughter, collected on scraps of paper from relations and friends. The principle remains the same, but the communication systems change with the times. My sisters and I are quickly getting into the habit of swopping recipes by fax, and Clémence, my 9-year-old niece, makes us all feel very old when she jots down a recipe dictated over the phone to try it for herself.

This book is about French home cooking as I know it – the way my family cooked. My cuisine grand-mère is based on family recipes that I started collecting, and experimenting with, nearly twenty years ago. Cooking proper began for me after leaving Oxford when I was let loose on my first kitchen in a basement flat in Shepherds Bush. My first graduate dinner party was a mitigated success. I scalded my ankle when I dropped a dish of braised celery (no one saw the mishap, so back into the dish went the wretched vegetable). The evening was saved by Madeleine's pommes meringuées, a gorgeous triple-layered combination of tart apple slices at the bottom, thick, sweet crème pâtissière in the middle and crisp meringue on top.

Recipes in a family network are never particularly precise – a little glass of this and a handful of that, a pinch of this and two fingers' width of that – but battles can rage between relatives and friends about their different versions of the same dish. Do you really put mushrooms in your bœuf bourguignon, cheese in your quiche lorraine, croutons around your blanquette de veau? If the dish is a success, the argument is forgotten and the revised version of the recipe – or some particularly good trick – may make its way in due course into a new set of files.

Cuisine grand-mère is not about authenticity at all cost. It always errs on the side of practicality. It loves making do, with the help of little twists that work well, clever *trucs*, not-so-secret family secrets proudly and willingly shared with others. It assumes that the recipients are not absolute beginners, but have a clue about basic techniques, enough common sense and a touch of flair. Given these not unreasonable assumptions, it is friendly and sensible, not aimed at experts, but at amateurs who have to cook regularly and might as well get some satisfaction from it.

Sometimes it will cut corners, especially when it comes to daunting complex classics with dozens of obscure ingredients. Sensible editing takes place: The chances are – outside the southwest of France – that a family *cassoulet* will not quite be the 'real' thing, whatever that may be. But it will be practical and will probably taste all right even if you are hundreds of miles from the Castelnaudary market. Last but not least it will not be extravagant.

Thrift is an important part of the *grand-mère* approach. My own grandmother enjoyed telling us, three-quarters jokingly, that we were lucky to have both butter and jam on our *tartines*: it wasn't like that in her day, one or the other, yes, but not both. That was a matter of principle.

Cheaper cuts of meat are simmered for a long time, variety meat tackled uncompromisingly, vegetables and seasonal produce feature prominently when at their best and cheapest. I remember the astonishment on an American boyfriend's face when he was formally served a summer dinner of boiled egg (one or two, on request), followed by a mountain of *haricots verts* from the garden, tender, buttered

The main approach to Fourchettes

and garlicky. Then came a local *Cendré* goat cheese and, at the last, a large dish of strawberries, picked that afternoon, served with *crème fraîche* in honour of our guest. He asked me if my grandmother was a vegetarian – this was in the early Seventies, before vegetarian became a household word.

In the Seventies and during most of the Eighties, poor old *cuisine grand-mère* took quite a knocking. It was eclipsed by the clean lines and sharp colours of *nouvelle cuisine*. It lost the battle in bistros and homes *à la mode* (*grand-mère*, in any case, never claimed to be the cuisine of top restaurants), but patiently waited for the wheel to turn and upstart *nouvelle* to lose its youthful charm. And, after two decades, the age of *cuisine grand-mère* has clearly come again. Fashionable chefs everywhere are confiding that they have rediscovered the joys and values of *cuisine traditionnelle* (the expensive, professional relative of both *grand-mère* and its fundamentalist country cousin, *cuisine du terroir*), while remembering the strong points of *nouvelle* – lightness, apparent simplicity and the use of the best possible ingredients.

The good-natured *grand-mère* approach is nothing if not flexible. It has reacted well to this new challenge, lost a few calories, worked on its looks and adopted some new tricks. Once again it is comfortably reigning in French kitchens – even if recipes have to be faxed during the cook's office hours.

Cuisine grand-mère is old-fashioned by definition. It assumes that the cook's place is in the house – not necessarily at the stove, but at hand: to give the pot a quick stir, add a few mushrooms twenty minutes before serving, then finish off the sauce with a nifty liaison. Rather than great skills, it requires a little attention and a presence. In the 1990s it makes perfect weekend cooking – relaxing but fiddly enough to be satisfying for the person who enjoys cooking. And it is ideal for the growing number of people who are choosing to work from home – what could be nicer than abandoning the desk for five minutes' creative puttering in the kitchen?

The end result will be satisfying, too: there is nothing particularly *légère* about *cuisine grand-mère*. I have tried to make my recipes as light as possible without altering their character and have given options whenever I can. This was not too difficult an exercise as, perhaps not altogether by accident, thrifty often coincides with healthy in the *grand-mère* style as I know it. First course salads and vegetables are used in abundance and sweet desserts kept for special occasions. By tradition, butter, cream and eggs are ingredients you are supposed to be reasonably economical with. Flour I use sparingly. Waste not, want not: this is not stinginess, but just good old household management. The French spend a great deal more of their income on food than the English or Americans, but they believe in spending their money wisely.

One other cost-conscious lesson that I try to heed is to make leftovers palatable – I am not saying that I use them creatively, because the idea of stretching *les restes* to the limit makes me shudder. Old habits die hard, however. As I write I am recovering from a surfeit of leftover Easter *gigot*. It was a joy served cold at the next meal, with a good garlic mayonnaise, and still pretty good the day after as a spicy *hachis parmentier* under a layer of creamed potato. But what was I to do on the third day? There was still a lot of *gigot* left. Well, I hesitated and looked at it, and thought of stuffed tomatoes and hesitated again. In the end, the dog Dickie had a great supper.

A cave sitting room with frescoes

POSTSCRIPT

IT IS NOW ten years since I wrote *Cuisine Grand-Mère*. Looking back over the decade, I take stock of the spirit of the time. A passion for food and all things to do with food has swept the Western world, both old and new. Chefs have eclipsed photographers and hairdressers as media darlings, television stars and gossip column fodder. My professional world of food magazine journalism has been hit by commercial realism. Anything to do with food must now have a spin, a marketing plan or sponsors with deep pockets. (The concept of spin was unheard of in 1990: let's hope that it is but a flash in the pan. In French, a spinning top is a *toupie* and *têtes de toupie*, people with heads like spinning tops, are notoriously dizzy and forgetful.) The age of culinary innocence may appear to be in danger of disappearing.

What most threatens culinary integrity in France is an epidemic of fast-food outlets. My 8-year-old niece Juliette, one of the aforementioned and now quite grownup Clémence's two little sisters, recently insisted on a McDonald's lunch after a morning's travels around London with a doting but unamused aunt. On her first visit to this strange big city, the red and yellow *M* shone like a reassuring beacon. She

Lotte à la Provençale

- 750g de lotte
- 4 tomates ou 1 petite boite
- 2 gros oignons
- 1 gousse d'ail
- 1 verre de vin blanc sec
- 6 cuillerées à soupe d'huile d'olive
- 50g de fromage râpé
- persil, thym, romarin, sel, poivre,

Coupez la lotte en morceaux. Faites-la revenir vivement à la poêle dans la moitié de l'huile d'olive avec l'oignon haché. Très vite la lotte deviendra plus ferme et d'un blanc doré. Retirez-la de la poêle, disposez-la dans un

T.S.V.P

Monkfish

Gratin dauphinois

- 750g de p. de terre
- 2 oeufs
- ½ litre lait
- 1 gousse d'ail
- sel, poivre
- 50g de beurre

Coupez les p. de terre en rondelles assez fines. Disposez-les par rangées dans un plat à terre, préalablement frotté avec une gousse d'ail puis beurré. Faites tiédir le lait, battez-y les oeufs avec sel, poivre et un peu muscade. Versez ce mélange sur les p. de terre. Ajoutez qq. morceaux de beurre à la surface. Cuisez à four chaud environ 45 mn.

Potato gratin

Gratin de Haddock au riz

pour 4 personnes

- 750g de filets de haddock
- 1l de lait
- 50g de fromage râpé
- 2 oeufs
- 250g riz
- sel, poivre, muscade, persil
- 50g de beurre ou margarine
- 3 cuillerées de chapelure

Lavez les filets de haddock, mettez-les à cuire à l'eau froide. Quand l'eau commence à bouillir, égouttez le haddock, remettez à cuire à l'eau froide, laissez frémir 5 minutes, égouttez, rincez puis bien enlevez la peau. X Puis mettez à égoutter le haddock dans 1l. de lait avec une cuillerée de beurre et

T.S.V.P

Smoked haddock

just had to have *un apimil au Macdo* (a request that puzzled me until I worked out the phonetics; parents of young children will be quicker to spot the happy meal phenomenon).

Yet all is not gloom and doom, even if you surrender children under the age of ten to Ronald McDonald. Later in the day, young Juliette helped prepare a proper lemony cream sauce, to serve with salmon fillets roasted in the oven. She then did it full justice. The next generation, in France at any rate, seems to have the ability to enjoy both fast food and good home cooking – *cuisine grand-mère*. Different foods for different occasions. It helps enormously that family meals, less frequent because of the increasing pressure of work on both parents, are still an institution. These meals tend to be simpler than in the past during the working week – not just because of the pressure of time, but also because eating healthily has emerged as an everyday priority. On birthdays and high days and holidays, families still gather around a table to enjoy food, drink and conversation. Calorie counts and fat contents are defied. Requests are made for what will be served at the next such occasion. Favourite dishes and past culinary triumphs are fondly evoked.

Mado's chocolate profiteroles, Tante Yonnée's lamb tagine, Anne-Sophie's terrines, Tata Boucher's sautéed potatoes . . . over the generations, my family goes on sharing a repertoire of dishes that entranced our taste buds and captured our imagination as children. Whenever I eat food prepared by my aunt, my sisters, or my cousins, there is always something uniquely familiar about it. In their hands even new recipes feel like old acquaintances. They are easy to remember and adopt. E-mails have replaced faxes (although not the backs of envelopes) as a means of swapping recipes, but we still speak the same culinary language. I am always surprised by how differently our generation, late thirties to just-turned fifty, rewrites our shared history. We remember the events and people of our childhood and adolescence very differently, but our foodie memories tend to be happy and have much in common. This must have a lot to do with the fact that our elders enjoyed their food, their wine and the rituals of family meals. Tempers may have flared and opinions differed, usually about politics, but not until after the main course. I remember my uncle Denis storming out of the dining room during a heated summer lunch sometime during the De Gaulle era. His dramatic exit took him no farther than the kitchen, where he was soon found happily enjoying second helpings and a glass of wine, care of Mado the peacemaker.

Mado is now well into her eighties, indomitably independent and living near Limoges, a compulsory detour for any member of the family who happens to be travelling to the southwest of France. Despite bad arthritis, she still sends my aunt Noëlle, her goddaughter, a home-baked cake every Christmas. She has remained the cheerful confidante of the family. Just as I used to listen to her in the kitchen, I ring her for news and gossip and sometimes to clarify details of family history. She asks me for updates about life in London and about my husband Colin, whom she only met twice, but approved of as if she had known him forever because of his *sens de l'humor très british*. She is keen to know about vacations in Saint-Malo in Brittany, our new vacation home.

Our time in the Touraine came to an end when my father died. After the well-known riches of the produce of the Loire valley, the trips to farmhouses for goat cheese, the wine tastings at local producers, the familiar combinations of ingredients, the move to Saint-Malo was a complete break. It immediately rejuvenated my enthusiasm for traditional home cooking and has resulted in a batch of new recipes in this book. It is a great joy and luxury to have a different local market to go to every day of the week. I write the names with a smile: Paramé, Dinard, Rocabey, Saint-Servan – they all offer fantastic fish and seafood, farmhouse poultry and salt-marsh lamb. There is always one stall selling hand-churned salty butter, slapped into shape for each customer. The vegetables can require a lot of scrubbing, particularly the mushrooms and the tiny nutty potatoes stall holders tend to keep under the table for people who know what to ask for, but their flavour is well worth the elbow grease.

More often than not, the unpredictable climate of Saint-Malo means that the kitchen is the best place to spend an afternoon, closely observed by Muscade, my brother-in-law's glossy black Labrador, helped or not by occasional skilled, or not-so-skilled, willing *sous-chefs* of various ages. The kind of cooking I do there is not so much complicated as considered. I take time to blanch ingredients, flavour stocks, finely chop shallots and herbs, simmer sauces patiently. The idea is to make the ingredients sing, not a grand opera, but a jolly *chanson*. In the spirit of *cuisine grand-mère*, I try to prepare dishes we will all enjoy eating and, who knows, dishes the next generation will remember.

beurre manié: mash together 1 teaspoon each of flour and soft butter. Divide into pellets and stir vigor-ously into hot sauces that need thickening over the heat.

butter: probably because I was brought up eating unsalted butter, I now really enjoy the taste of butter that is lightly salted. When a recipe does, however, demand soft unsalted butter, it is specified.

chicken stock: a light stock can easily be made by simmering the carcass, or at least some bones and gizzards, if possible, with a leek (or spring onion), carrot and bouquet garni (a sprig each of parsley and thyme and a bay leaf) for 30 minutes while you cook the meat. For a more elaborate method, see the *poule au pot* recipe (page 88). Chicken stock is worth having in the freezer.

chinois: a narrow strainer, extremely fine and a useful utensil to have.

citrus fruit: buy organic or unwaxed lemons and oranges, especially if you are going to zest them. If time allows, blanch strips of zest for a minute in boiling water before using.

crème fraîche: double cream with a dash of lemon makes a most acceptable substitute.

eggs: I use organic or free-range eggs, keep them in the refrigerator and ruthlessly throw away any unused eggs that are past their use-by date. And, without being pious about it, it is a good idea always to break eggs separately into a small bowl or saucer. The, albeit rare, occasions when an egg is bad invariably happen when you've just broken the last of the ten required for a mammoth meringue.

fish stock: the quickest of all stocks to make, with fish bones, prawns or other crustacean shells, simmered in water for 10 minutes with a bouquet garni. Avoid using the bones and trimmings of fatty fish such as salmon.

food processor: invaluable, particularly for non-pastry cooks, but takes a while to become second nature.

I am still using my faithful old Magimix *Cuisine Système 3000* and contemplating upgrading to a chrome-finish model I can leave permanently on display on the kitchen island. Choose a model that comes with a second smaller bowl, for everyday quick jobs.

garnish: I do not like the word. Think of it as a flourish; it should really add something to the dish – ideally a combination of zingy fresh flavour and visual appeal.

herbs: I use fresh herbs extravagantly and try to grow my own – with mixed success I have to say. As well as growing herbs, supermarkets sell packed herbs in little trays. Look for herbs packed in deeper trays, with as distant a sell-by date as possible. Keep in the refrigerator and cover with dampened paper towels after opening. Instead of letting them turn a stale yellow, finely chop leftover basil, parsley (including the stems), coriander, dill, chives and tarragon, and freeze in tiny freezer bags. Shake out straight from the freezer as needed and use again and again.

hollandaise sauce: I make mine in the food processor. bring to the boil 4 teaspoons of white wine vinegar or lemon juice with 3 tablespoons of water. Season with freshly ground black pepper and reduce the mixture to about 2 teaspoons. Melt 150 g unsalted butter in a separate saucepan until foamy – but do not let colour. Process 2 egg yolks with a small pinch of salt until smooth. Whizz in the reduced vinegar. With the machine on, trickle in the bubbling butter through the feed tube, a few drops at a time to begin with then a little faster as the sauce starts to emulsify. Continue until the sauce is smooth and thick. Check the seasoning and use as soon as possible – or keep for up to 30 minutes over warm water.

kitchen hygiene: I use a separate chopping board for raw meat and go through vast amounts of paper towels and disposable kitchen clothes. Dishcloths are put in a very hot wash and tend to have a very short life.

lardons: now sold in supermarkets. If you cannot find packed lardons in the freezer section, look for diced pancetta. We French have a word for it, *ventrèche* – a perfect alternative to lardons. Otherwise, ask your local favourite delicatessen or butcher to sell you bacon in thick, 2.5-cm slices. Cut into small dice. The flavour and crunch they add to salads, quiches and other dishes – lentils in particular – will be much greater than if you simply snip a standard bacon slice.

mayonnaise: hard-to-resist lovely mayonnaise can be made the slow painful way, by hand with a wooden spoon – or painlessly whizzed in the food processor. I tend to compromise with an electric mixer. Once you have made sure the ingredients and equipment are all at the same room temperature, and promised yourself that on no account will you speed up the process and pour in the oil too fast, there remains the familiar problem of having only two hands. One hand is to trickle in the oil and the other to hold the mixer. But what about the slippery bowl? I wedge it firmly in place on a mat of damp kitchen cloth.

As much as I like olive oil, I do not recommend using it on its own for mayonnaise – it will completely take over. Peanut oil on its own is extremely bland, so I use the mix below.

Serves 6
2 egg yolks
2 teaspoons wine vinegar (red or white)
a small pinch of salt
½ teaspoon Dijon mustard
150 ml peanut oil
120 ml light flavoured olive oil
TO SEASON
freshly ground black pepper
sea salt
lemon juice
TO FLAVOUR
finely chopped herbs – chervil, chives, parsley,
   tarragon or watercress
finely chopped garlic
finely chopped gherkins
anchovy essence

BRING ALL THE INGREDIENTS AND EQUIPMENT TO room temperature.

Beat the egg yolks until combined, then beat in the vinegar, salt and mustard. Whisking constantly, trickle in the peanut oil, literally drop by drop to begin, then a few drops at a time.

As soon as the mixture really appears to be thickening, trickle in the olive oil just a little more continuously, still whisking. Continue until you have incorporated both the peanut and olive oils.

Now taste the mayonnaise and season it with freshly ground black pepper, extra salt, if you like, and a little lemon juice. Beat in 1 tablespoon of boiling water, which will help the mayonnaise keep stable. Cover with plastic wrap and chill until needed. If you like, flavour to taste with some of the suggested additions.

microwave: I have one, but it stays idle except for the odd reheating job. My one and only microwave party trick is to use it to precook mushrooms before

frying or roasting, to get rid of excess moisture. Put them in a microwave dish, cover loosely and cook on high for 3 or 4 minutes. Drain well and use as required. You will be pleasantly surprised by the taste and texture. It is also good for wilting tomatoes before you add them to omelettes and other preparations. First pierce the skin or halve the tomatoes, then microwave, just like the mushrooms, for 2 or 3 minutes.

oil: for reasons of space, I limit the selection in my pantry. I keep sunflower oil, two kinds of olive oil and an everyday blend with a light flavour for cooking; and for salads and last-minute dousing I use a gutsy, extra-virgin olive oil. There are many brands and styles to experiment with. Walnut oil I only buy in small bottles and store in the refrigerator – it goes rancid very quickly, so don't keep it longer than 3 months.

paper towels: use liberally for drying ingredients and wiping hands, utensils and work surfaces.

peeling: in the recipes I assume that garlic and onions are peeled as a matter of course. If other vegetables require peeling, this is specified.

salad spinner: a wonderful gadget that collects all the moisture from salad leaves and saves a great deal of time and energy. A modest investment that I thoroughly recommend.

sauce blanche: white sauce. This quick recipe is a useful starting point for many variations. As well as the additions I suggest, also try mustard and capers. Béchamel sauce is made in exactly the same way, using milk instead of water. Flavour with tomato purée or cream and grated Gruyère cheese.

Serves 4
60 g butter
4 tablespoons flour
550 ml light stock or water
sea salt
freshly ground black pepper
TO ENRICH
30 g or more butter and/or the juice of 1 lemon
or 150 ml *crème fraîche*
or 1 egg yolk and 6 tablespoons single cream

IN A HEAVY-BASED SAUCEPAN, OVER A MODERATE heat, melt the butter, then stir in the flour, using a wooden spoon. Moisten at once with a little of the stock or water, stir to mix – from this stage on, I use a balloon whisk. Add the rest of the liquid, still stirring. Bring slowly to the boil, whisking very frequently, then reduce the heat and cook for several minutes – this is important, otherwise the sauce will taste floury. Season to taste with sea salt and freshly ground black pepper.

Enrich the sauce with 30 g or more butter and the juice of 1 lemon, or with 150 ml *crème fraîche* just before serving. Alternatively, in a small bowl combine 1 large egg yolk and 6 tablespoons single cream. Stir a little warm sauce into the egg and cream, then add to the pan and whisk in vigorously

over the heat. Keep whisking hard until the sauce becomes creamy.

sauté pan: like all French home cooks I use mine a great deal.

scissors: I keep several pairs of kitchen scissors and use them constantly, for snipping fresh herbs, spring onions, bacon slices, etc. In the interests of hygiene, the scissors used for snipping raw meats are a different colour.

sea salt: it tastes better than ordinary salt and you need less of it. The texture of coarse kosher salt is particularly pleasant.

shortcuts: in my experience, the French have always believed in using little tricks to make life easier and are no puritans when it comes to shortcuts in the kitchen. Convenience is not necessarily a dirty word. I use a lot of prepared salads and I have to admit I sometimes buy chilled pastry and meat stocks: expensive, but money well spent when you are a gourmande in a hurry.

spatula: a good spatula should be heatproof and flexible. It is not an easy thing to find. The best one I ever had was a present from an American friend and I have never found its like elsewhere.

things to bring back from France: the list varies from year to year. My current shopping list includes small blue-green *lentilles du Puy*, bitter dark chocolate, *saucisson*, small cans of extra-fine flageolets, *petits pois*, sugared ground almonds, tarragon mustard, caramels made with salted butter and incredibly buttery miniature Britanny biscuits, to give to friends. I no longer bring back cheeses, because most will not mature well after a bout of travelling.

timing: I find that even if I follow a recipe to the letter, the exact timing mysteriously varies from one occasion to the next. Always keep an eye on the progress and be prepared to take action and turn the heat up, down or off sooner – or later – than expected.

tomato *coulis:* a thin, strained purée of the juice and pulp of either canned or preferably fresh ripe tomatoes. *Coulis* is infinitely better than tomato purée and much used in the French kitchen – and mine.

vinaigrette: often too acidic. Use only top-quality vinegar and oil. A good basic vinaigrette is made with 1 tablespoon of red wine vinegar, 5 tablespoons of peanut oil, a tiny quantity of mustard and a generous seasoning of sea salt and pepper. Stir vigorously with a small sauce whisk.

If like me, you eat large quantities of salad and like a thick and emulsified vinaigrette, follow my uncle Jean's method. Blend or process together 100 ml red wine vinegar, 600 ml peanut oil, 1 tablespoon of strong Dijon mustard, 2 teaspoons of salt and plenty of freshly ground black pepper. Check the seasoning and refrigerate for 1 hour, then blend or process again. Refrigerate in a tightly closed, impeccably clean jar. This vinaigrette will keep for up to 3 weeks.

vinegars: too many bottles crowd kitchen shelves and gather dust. Since a little vinegar goes a long way, buy the more expensive brands. I tend to keep a bottle or two of good wine vinegars, sherry vinegar and balsamic and cider vinegars.

Potages
Soups

A LARGE WHITE CHINA tureen in the centre of the table, fragrant steam, deep plates full of velvety goodness – my early memories of soup are of contentment and a feeling that things were as they should be and had always been. The curtains were drawn against the winter night, a clock was ticking somewhere. I was sharing an evening meal with my father's parents, *Bon-Papa* and *Bonne-Maman*, a quietly happy couple at peace with the world.

In France, as elsewhere, soup for a long time was the only dish at the last meal of the day. Hence the verb *souper,* which meant just what it said – to take evening soup – centuries before it went upmarket to describe a late, light meal. Soup in French homes has remained an evening rather than a lunchtime dish, starter or main course, perhaps not quite as popular as it used to be, but making a distinct comeback now that more and more kitchens are equipped with that magic *robot,* the food processor. It seems that once again soup is good for you.

Soupe or *potage?* Most French people will tell you that the words are synonymous, but if you delve into it, *potage* turns out to be rather more refined, implying culinary skills, the use of a strainer, or the making of a liaison. Soup started life humbly as a slice of stale bread over which hot liquid was poured. It has remained part of the French experience every bit as much as cheese: some decades ago Curnonsky listed more than five hundred varieties of *soupes* and *potages,* from starry kitchens to farmhouses.

Soup is flexible and accommodating – the only thing it does suffer from is not being served hot enough. As I like a good, substantial soup, but not buckets of it, I have generally allowed in the recipes about 1.2 litres liquid for 4 servings. This is only a guideline, as many factors influence the water content of any given vegetable. Feel free to vary and add a little extra water, stock or cream if the soup seems too thick – or if you have an extra guest. Soup is a dish that can usually be stretched to go a little further.

Potage au Potiron
Pumpkin Soup

With the exception of courgettes, the favoured baby of the family, gourds and squashes do not feature very highly on the list of prized French vegetables. Pumpkins, in particular, have a lowly status and are often regarded as cattle fodder. However, they are discreetly put to very good use in a number of tasty, country-style soups, like my autumnal favourite here.

Serves 4

450 g wedge of pumpkin
2 large ripe tomatoes
1 large white onion
60 g butter
1 scant tablespoon sugar
1.2 litres milk
sea salt
freshly ground black pepper
4 tablespoons single cream
a few sprigs of parsley
croutons, to serve

Remove the skin and seeds from the pumpkin and dice the flesh. Blanch, skin and seed the tomatoes, then chop the flesh. Coarsely chop the onion. In a large, heavy-based saucepan, melt half the butter. Then stir in the vegetables and cook for a couple of minutes. Sprinkle in the sugar and add a small glass of water. Cover and cook gently for about 30 minutes, or until all the vegetables are soft.

Meanwhile, bring the milk to the boil in a suitable saucepan; keep hot. Add half the milk to the cooked vegetables and blend, using a blender or food processor, then pour the mixture into the pan with the remaining hot milk and whisk in. Alternatively, push the purée through a strainer into the hot milk and whisk in vigorously until well combined.

Season to taste with salt and freshly ground black pepper, then stir in the cream. Keep the soup hot over a gentle heat. Snip the parsley. Just before serving, whisk in the remaining butter.

Sprinkle the croutons and the snipped parsley over the soup and serve.

Soupe au Pistou
Vegetable Soup with Basil, Garlic and Cheese

PISTOU IS WHAT GENOA'S *pesto* becomes along the coast, on the French side of the border. This big, generous soup is well worth the entire crop of a kitchen pot of basil. Followed by a lightly dressed green salad, some cheese and a little fruit, it makes a good *plat unique* supper. And it has the advantage of being unobtrusively vegetarian – a good dish to serve to a mixed party. The meat eaters won't miss their fix.

350 g small white haricot beans
2 medium-size potatoes
350 g French beans
350 g courgettes
2 carrots
2 leeks
1 turnip
sea salt

Serves 6 to 8

freshly ground black pepper
120 g small macaroni

FOR THE *PISTOU* SAUCE
2 ripe tomatoes
4 to 6 cloves of garlic
120 g of fresh basil leaves
120 g freshly grated Parmesan
100 ml olive oil
60 g grated Gruyère cheese, to
　serve

SOAK THE HARICOT BEANS FOR AT LEAST 6 hours. Drain, rinse and drain again. Put in a saucepan, pour in 2 litres cold water and bring to the boil. Skim if necessary.

Prepare the other vegetables. Peel and chop the potatoes; top and tail the beans, then cut into segments; slice the courgettes; scrape or peel the carrots; slice and wash the leeks; peel and chop the turnip. Ensure the pieces are no larger than 4 cm.

After 45 minutes add the vegetables to the pan, cover and simmer for 45 minutes, or until tender. Season with salt and freshly ground black pepper. Add the macaroni and finish cooking the soup, uncovered.

Meanwhile, prepare the *pistou* sauce. Blanch, skin, seed and chop the tomatoes. Using a large mortar and pestle, pound the garlic, then add the basil leaves and pound well. Work in the chopped tomatoes and half the Parmesan, then add the olive oil a little at a time, mixing it in as for a mayonnaise. Alternatively, combine everything in the food processor, taking care not to over-process the sauce. Stir 1 ladleful of the soup liquid into the sauce, then pour into the soup and leave to settle and infuse for a few minutes over a low heat. Combine the remaining Parmesan with the Gruyère and serve in a bowl at the same time as the soup.

Potage Saint-Germain
Fresh Pea Soup

A DELICATE PEA SOUP flavoured with chervil. The Saint-Germain in question is the Comte de Saint-Germain, Louis XV's war minister, whose name blesses preparations involving peas. Reduce the amount of water to 250 ml in the recipe below, go easy on the blending and, voilà, you have purée Saint-Germain, a good accompaniment to fish and veal.

1 kg fresh baby garden peas, in
   the pod
hearts of 3 lettuces
12 button onions
several sprigs of chervil

Serves 4

a few sprigs of parsley
90 g butter

1 small egg yolk
4 tablespoons single cream
sea salt
freshly ground black pepper
small croutons, to serve

SHELL THE PEAS, SHRED THE LETTUCE hearts, chop the onions and snip the fresh herbs. In a large, heavy-based saucepan, melt 60 g butter, then add the vegetables and herbs and cook gently for 5 minutes, stirring frequently.

Pour in 1.2 litres boiling water and simmer for 20 to 30 minutes, until the vegetables are very tender. Reserving 2 to 3 tablespoons of peas, transfer the vegetables and most of the liquid to a blender or food processor. Blend until smooth and return to the pan. Alternatively, push through a fine strainer, mashing the vegetables well with the back of a wooden spoon to extract as much pulp as possible. Whisk the liquid and purée until well combined.

Reheat gently. Combine the egg yolk and cream in a small bowl and stir in a little soup, then gradually add this liaison to the pan, stirring well. Season to taste with salt and freshly ground black pepper. Just before serving, stir in the reserved peas, whisk in the remaining butter and add the croutons.

Soupe aux Lentilles
Lentil Soup

Lentils seem to be to the early 1990s what the kiwi fruit was to the previous decade – and after years of neglect, it is now a case of lentils with practically everything. As a lifelong loyal supporter of this legume, I am delighted to see them back in fashion. For me, no trip to France is complete without the purchase of at least one package of dark green, little *lentilles du Puy*. They cook quickly and cleanly, without disintegrating into an unappetizing mush and they have a good strong flavour.

450 g small dark green lentils
2 tablespoons olive oil, plus
    extra for serving, if wished
30 g butter, plus extra for
    serving, if wished
1 large onion
1 clove of garlic
1 large potato

Serves 6

1 carrot
1 thick-cut slice of smoked
    bacon, without the rind
1 bouquet garni
1 tablespoon tomato purée
sea salt
freshly ground black pepper

Rinse the lentils well and soak them for 10 minutes in cold water. Meanwhile, gently heat the oil and butter in a large, heavy-based saucepan and prepare the vegetables.

Chop the onion and garlic; peel and chop the potato; scrape or peel and then slice the carrot. Sauté the onion in the pan until browned, then add the drained lentils and the vegetables.

Chop up the bacon and add to the pan. Stir until everything is well mixed.

Add the bouquet garni and about 1.5 litres cold water to the pan. Bring gently to the boil and simmer for about 30 minutes, or until the lentils and vegetables are cooked and soft. Remove the bouquet garni. Reserving about 2 ladlefuls, blend the soup in a blender or food processor. Return to the pan and stir in the reserved unblended mixture and the tomato purée. If the soup looks too thick, thin it down with a cup of boiling water.

Season to taste with salt and freshly ground black pepper. Serve piping hot. You might like to add a trickle of olive oil or a knob of butter to each bowl of soup.

Any leftover soup will keep very nicely in the refrigerator for a couple of days – just remember to add a little extra liquid when reheating.

Gratinée au Roquefort
Onion Soup with Roquefort

A CHEESE LOVER'S version of the celebrated soup. It is gutsy, simple and effective – a good dish to
'delegate' to would-be helping hands, but make sure they don't burn the onions.
For a luxurious finishing touch, try spooning a little liaison of egg yolk and cream into each bowl, between
the top crust and the soup. Definitely not home fare as I remember it,
but recently enjoyed in a London restaurant.

Serves 4

750 g large white onions
90 g butter
2 teaspoons flour
sea salt
freshly ground black pepper
a little nutmeg, grated or
    ground
2 to 3 tablespoons brandy
120 g Roquefort cheese
8 to 12 thin slices French
    bread, lightly toasted
30 g Gruyère cheese

SLICE THE ONIONS. IN A LARGE, HEAVY-based saucepan, melt the butter and gently sauté the onion slices until soft, without letting them colour. Sprinkle the flour over the onions and stir it in well. Pour in 1.2 litres boiling water and cook for 15 to 20 minutes. Heat the oven to 200°C/Gas 6. Season the soup with salt, freshly ground black pepper, a little nutmeg and then the brandy.

Mash the Roquefort with a fork. Reserve 4 slices of French bread and spread the mashed Roquefort over the rest. Arrange the coated bread in individual ovenproof bowls, then pour in the soup.

Place a slice of the reserved bread on top of each serving, then grate the Gruyère over the tops.

Brown the toppings in the oven for about 10 minutes. Serve at once.

Potage à l'Oseille
Sorrel Soup

FRESH, GREEN AND a little sharp, this is a lovely spring soup. Once the sorrel season is over, I use exactly the same method to make watercress or spinach soup.

450 g sorrel
30 g butter
2 potatoes
1 egg yolk

Serves 4

90 ml double cream
sea salt
freshly ground black pepper

WASH, TRIM AND ROUGHLY SHRED THE sorrel leaves. In a large, heavy-based saucepan, melt the butter. Add the sorrel leaves and gently stew for a few minutes.

Peel the potatoes and cut into roughly 2.5-cm dice. Add to the sorrel, then pour in 1.2 litres cold water, bring to the boil and cook for 10 to 15 minutes more.

In a small bowl, combine the egg yolk and the cream, stirring in the cream gradually.

Transfer the soup mixture to a blender or food processor, reserving a few tablespoons of the liquid and blend the soup.

Stir the reserved liquid into the egg and cream. Return the soup to the pan, then gradually add the egg and cream, whisking well. Season to taste, then reheat until very hot, but do not boil.

Potage Bonne Femme
Leek, Carrot and Potato Soup

A SIMPLE AND comforting soup. I have tried finishing it off with a dollop of *crème fraîche*, but have gone back to using butter, which somehow always tastes better with this combination of root vegetables.

2 waxy potatoes
3 large leeks
4 carrots
90 g butter, plus extra for
  serving

Serves 4

a few sprigs of fresh thyme
2 bay leaves
1 or 2 cloves of garlic, peeled
sea salt
freshly ground black pepper

PEEL THE POTATOES. WASH AND TRIM THE leeks, then scrape or peel the carrots. Chop the vegetables into roughly 2.5-cm cubes. In a heavy-based saucepan, melt half the butter, then sauté the vegetables until lightly coloured. Add the thyme, bay leaves and garlic to the vegetables, then pour in about 1.2 litres boiling water. Simmer for about 30 minutes.

When the vegetables are cooked, blend the soup in the blender or food processor. Season to taste with salt and freshly ground black pepper. Serve piping hot, with a good knob of butter in each bowl.

Soupe au Poivron et à la Tomate
Roasted Red Pepper and Tomato Soup

B<small>RIGHT RED, GUTSY</small> and fresh tasting. Serve chilled on a hot day.

Serves 4 to 6

3 red peppers
6 large ripe tomatoes
75 ml fruity olive oil
3 cloves of garlic, halved
sea salt
freshly ground black pepper
1 teaspoon sugar

leaves from a few sprigs of
   thyme and oregano or
   1 teaspoon each of dried
   thyme and oregano
600 ml chicken or vegetable
   stock
6–9 black olives
¼ baguette

H<small>EAT THE OVEN TO</small> 200°C/G<small>AS</small> 6. H<small>ALVE</small> the peppers and remove the seeds and white membranes. Halve the tomatoes and scoop out the seeds and excess pulp. Brush a baking tin with half the olive oil, add the garlic cloves, reserving half a clove and place the peppers on top of the garlic, cut sides down. Roast for about 10 minutes, then add the tomatoes, cut sides down. Season the tomatoes and sprinkle with the sugar, thyme and oregano, reserving a few leaves. Roast for 15 minutes, until charred and bubbly. Leave to cool a little, then peel the peppers.

Whiz the peppers and tomatoes with their pan juices in a food processor and tip into a saucepan. Add the stock to the food processor and whiz briefly, then add to the saucepan. Adjust the seasoning and reheat over a low heat until piping hot. Alternatively, chill for at least 2 hours to serve cold.

Stone and chop the olives. Put in a cup and sprinkle with the rest of the olive oil and herbs, mix and set aside or chill until needed.

Cut the bread into thin slices, rub with the cut side of the garlic and toast under a hot grill.

To serve, distribute the olive mixture between the croutons. Ladle the soup into suitable shallow bowls. Float a few olive croutons over each helping.

Vichyssoise aux Asperges et Fines Herbes

Asparagus and Herb Vichyssoise

Asparagus prices vary enormously – this is a soup I make as soon as the precious stalks have lost their early season novelty appeal, when their cost has come down to that of run-of-the-mill vegetables. This is not a difficult dish to make, but its texture and appearance will be much enhanced if you (a) conscientiously prepare the asparagus, removing all the strings (especially if you are using fat, white stalks) and (b) sweat the onions over a very low heat to prevent them from browning. Consume hot or chilled, depending on the weather. When I serve this vichyssoise chilled, these days I often finish it with thick plain yogurt rather than cream, but *yaourt* definitely did not feature in my original recipe.

	Serves 4	
the white parts of 4 large spring onions 1 large potato 500 g asparagus 45 g butter 1.2 litres chicken stock (see page 12)		several sprigs each of tarragon and chives a small bunch of parsley sea salt freshly ground black pepper 120 ml single cream (or a mixture of cream and yogurt, see above)

Prepare the vegetables. Peel and finely slice the spring onions. Peel and chop the potato. Carefully trim the asparagus, discarding any tough woody ends and peeling off any knobby, stringy bits; cut and reserve the tips of 4 to 12 stalks (depending on size), then cut the remaining stalks into segments.

In a large, heavy-based saucepan, melt the butter over a low heat. Add the sliced onions and sweat for a few minutes, stirring frequently and keeping the heat low so the onions do not colour. Add the chopped potato and continue stirring for a few minutes, still over a low heat.

Add the asparagus segments to the onions and potato, pour in the stock and gently bring to a simmer. Snip half the tarragon, chives and parsley into the mixture and season lightly with salt and freshly ground black pepper. Now cover and simmer gently for about 20 minutes until the asparagus and

potato are soft. Add the reserved asparagus tips after about 15 minutes. Remove the asparagus tips from the pan and set aside after cooking. Leave the soup to cool for a few minutes, then purée. If the texture looks less than perfectly smooth, press the soup through a fine strainer. Check the seasoning.

If serving hot, pour the soup back into the pan, stir in the cream and heat through gently. Snip the remaining herbs and stir them into the soup, then add the reserved asparagus tips at the last minute.

If serving chilled, stir in half the cream and 4 tablespoons of cold water – the soup tends to thicken as it gets cold. Leave the soup until cold and refrigerate for at least 2 hours or until needed. Also chill the reserved asparagus tips. Just before serving, check the seasoning, snip in the remaining herbs and stir. Swirl in the remaining cream and plop in a few ice cubes, then add the asparagus tips.

Soupe Fraîche aux Epinards et à l'Avocat
Chilled Spinach and Avocado Soup

WHENEVER I CAN find baby spinach and decent avocados in the market at the same time, usually for a month or so in the early summer – and sometimes again at the very end of that season – this soup features regularly on the menu. The nutty smoothness of the avocado combines well with the slightly peppery sharpness of the spinach.

750 g young tender spinach
sea salt
3 ripe, blemish-free avocados
2 or 3 lemons

Serves 4

a few sprigs of flat-leaf parsley
600 ml chilled chicken stock
hot-pepper sauce, cayenne
    pepper or harissa

DISCARD THE SPINACH STEMS AND ANY large ribs. Blanch in lightly salted boiling water for a couple of minutes; drain. Meanwhile, skin and chop the avocados. Transfer them to a blender or food processor, squeeze the lemons and add the juice, then the wilted spinach. Snip the parsley and add to the avocado and spinach mixture; blend until smooth. Add the stock and blend again.

Transfer to a large bowl. Season to taste with salt and a little hot-pepper sauce, cayenne pepper or harissa.

Gradually whisk in about 450 ml water and perhaps a little extra lemon juice, until the soup has a nice consistency.

Refrigerate for at least 1 hour or until needed. Adjust the seasoning.

Serve the soup with a couple of ice cubes in each bowl.

Velouté aux Champignons
Creamy Mushroom Soup

OBSERVANT READERS WILL notice that this is one of the few times that I use chicken stock in a soup recipe instead of plain *château la pompe* (water from the faucet). The reason is that it makes a big difference to the flavour of the dish – one of those occasions when faking it with a stock cube just won't do.

Which type of mushroom to use? Any cultivated, very fresh mushrooms will give of their best in this recipe. At the moment I am favouring brown cap *champignons de Paris*. If you feel extravagant, follow a great *gourmand's* advice: Curnonsky concludes his splendidly creamy version of *potage aux champignons* with the observation that the soup 'will obviously taste better with wild mushrooms'.

Serves 4

450 g fresh mushrooms
½ lemon
90 g butter, plus extra to finish
50 g flour

1.2 litres chicken stock (see page 12)

1 or 2 egg yolks
100 ml double cream
sea salt
freshly ground black pepper

WIPE AND TRIM THE MUSHROOMS. KEEP aside 90 g and very finely chop the rest. Finely grate the zest of the lemon, then squeeze the juice, reserving both.

In a large, heavy-based saucepan, make a roux. Melt 60 g of the butter, stir in the flour and cook gently for a couple of minutes, stirring constantly. Gradually pour in the chicken stock, a little at a time, stirring continuously and vigorously to prevent lumps forming, then add the chopped mushrooms and bring to the boil, still stirring. Reduce the heat and add the lemon juice and zest. Cook gently for 20 to 25 minutes, stirring frequently.

Meanwhile, slice the reserved mushrooms very finely and sauté in the remaining butter. In a small bowl, combine the egg yolk or yolks with the cream. Stir in a ladleful of the soup liquid, then gradually pour the mixture into the pan, always stirring well; keep hot, but not boiling. Add the sautéed mushroom slices.

Season to taste with salt and a little freshly ground black pepper. Whisk in a good knob of butter and serve piping hot.

Hors d'Œuvre
Appetisers

No French family lunch is complete without some little *hors d'œuvre*, or light first course, a clever starter that somehow simultaneously whets the appetite, yet takes the edge off it, while giving the cook a few extra minutes to organise the main dish. Most *hors d'œuvre* are as easy on the cook as they are appetising: many favourites need very little preparation indeed. What could be simpler to assemble than a few slices of *saucisson*, some black olives and wedges of hard-boiled eggs? The dish welcomes you to the table without being in the least fussy.

My sister, Françoise, recently dampened my enthusiastic *hors d'œuvre* reminiscences by pointing out that the slices of *saucisson* were carefully counted and preprandial looting severely monitored. How could I forget . . . *saucissons*, expensive and, even in a less health-conscious decade, not known for their dietary qualities, never lasted long in our house. More often than not, the *saucisson* ration was accompanied by a substantial fresh salad. This varied subtly according to the people sitting around the table. It could be marinated mushrooms when a friend of our mother came to lunch, creamy cucumber for grandparents and older relatives, or celery root mayonnaise on the rare occasions our father managed to get away from the office. And if it was 'just us', something like plain grated carrots or shredded cabbage would be the order of the day.

SALADE D'ENDIVE ET DE POIRE AU ROQUEFORT

Chicory and Pear Salad with Roquefort

I STILL REMEMBER THE first time I tasted the exciting combination of tender sweet pear, slightly bitter chicory and pungent Roquefort some years ago, in Brives in southwest France. I was mixing business and pleasure during a book fair. This salad works just as well before or after the main course.

	Serves 4	
6 heads of chicory, red or white, rinsed and drained		FOR THE DRESSING
2 ripe pears		1½ tablespoons sunflower oil
a little lemon juice for brushing		1½ tablespoons walnut oil
100 g Roquefort cheese		2 teaspoons red wine vinegar
		sea salt
		freshly ground black pepper

SEPARATE THE CHICORY LEAVES AND CHOP the large leaves. Halve and core the pears. Peel them if you like, brush with lemon juice and slice thinly. Whisk the dressing ingredients together in a large, shallow bowl.

Toss the leaves in the dressing, then fold in the pear slices. Adjust the seasoning. Cut the Roquefort cheese into slivers and don't worry if it crumbles a little.

Arrange the endive and pear slices on individual plates and place the Roquefort cheese on top. Season with extra pepper.

ROUILLE

Provençal Hot-Pepper Sauce

ROUILLE GETS ITS name from its attractive rust colour and its fieriness from small, red-hot peppers. With *tapenade* and *anchoïade* (see page 35), it makes an appetising trilogy. Serve with an assortment of raw vegetables, steamed or boiled small new potatoes, or spread on warm toast.

	Serves 4	
2 small red chilli peppers		sea salt
1 small slice day-old white bread, crust removed	2 cloves of garlic	1 teaspoon tomato purée
a little milk	1 egg yolk	100 ml olive oil
		cayenne pepper, if wished

DISCARD THE STEMS AND SEEDS OF THE chillies (soak dried chillies in cold water first for a few hours). Soak the bread in a little milk, then squeeze to get rid of excess milk.

Using a blender, food processor or mortar and pestle, combine the chillies, garlic, milky bread, egg yolk, salt and tomato purée. Add the oil, a little at a time, until the mixture is very thick and smooth. Thin it out with a dash of cold water. Check the seasoning – if it's not hot enough for you, sprinkle cayenne pepper over the mixture.

Poireaux Vinaigrette
Leek Salad

THE POOR MAN'S asparagus, the modest leek, really responds to being treated like its posh cousin. It is important to dress the leeks while they are still warm to let the flavours combine and this starter is best eaten *tiède* – just above room temperature.

750 g fairly slim leeks
sea salt
a few sprigs of chives

Serves 4

FOR THE VINAIGRETTE
1 small hard-boiled egg
1 tablespoon Dijon mustard
sea salt
freshly ground black pepper
2 teaspoons white wine
   vinegar
90 ml peanut oil

CUT OFF THE BEARDED ROOTS OF THE leeks and the tough end of the green tops. Slit the whole length of each leek with a sharp knife and discard any discoloured top layers. Gently open the leeks and rinse well under cold running water. Tie the leeks in bunches of 3 or 4 and cook in boiling salted water for 8 to 10 minutes. Transfer to a large strainer or colander and drain well.

While the leeks are cooking, prepare the vinaigrette. Grate the hard-boiled egg into a small bowl and mash with the mustard. Add a pinch of salt and a sprinkling of freshly ground black pepper, then stir in the vinegar and oil. Beat until well combined.

Gently squeeze the warm leeks with a very clean towel to remove excess moisture. Arrange the leeks on a dish like asparagus and pour the vinaigrette over them, then snip the chives and scatter them on top. Sprinkle a little extra pepper over the dish at the last minute and eat while still warm.

Salade de Poivrons à l'Avocat
Sweet Red Pepper and Avocado Salad

THIS COLOURFUL LITTLE starter has been a family favourite ever since avocados lost their *de luxe* dinner-party status and became staple fare for much of the year. Skinning peppers is a tedious task, so once I get going I always char more than I need for the salad; marinated peppers mature nicely in the refrigerator for a week or so. After a few days, you'll have a deep, piquant-sweet mixture that makes a good pasta sauce. Marinated peppers also do wonders for plain chicken pieces. Skin the chicken pieces, coat with the mixture and season generously with black pepper. Bake for 30 to 45 minutes, in a 130°C/Gas ½ oven, basting once.

Serves 4 to 6

3 ripe, unblemished red
  peppers
90 ml good strong-flavoured
  olive oil
2 ripe avocados
1 lemon
sea salt
freshly ground black pepper
crusty bread, to serve

WASH AND DRY THE PEPPERS, THEN CHAR them. I do that under the grill, cursing quietly as I burn my fingers, turning the peppers until all the surfaces are charred and blistered. Leave them until cool enough to handle, then remove the skins – they will peel off easily if the peppers are charred enough. Don't worry about small stubborn patches of skin – the marinade will soften them. Cut the peppers in half lengthways and carefully remove the seeds, cores and membranes. Slice into narrow strips and cut each strip into 2 or 3 segments. Put the peppers in a bowl, coat with the olive oil, cover with plastic wrap and chill for at least 12 hours, during which time the mixture should be stirred once or twice.

Just before serving, halve the avocados and remove the stones and skins. Cut into thin slices, squeeze the lemon and moisten the avocados well with the juice. Combine with two-thirds of the marinated peppers and their juices, reserving the rest.

Season with a very little salt and more generously with black pepper. Serve with crusty fresh bread.

CHAMPIGNONS EN SALADE
Mushroom Salad

THIS LIGHTLY MARINATED salad makes a neat, fresh little starter and is a good way of making the most of not-very-exciting cultivated mushrooms. It will keep well for a couple of days in the refrigerator.

350 g fresh white button
  mushrooms
1½ lemons
4 tablespoons olive oil

Serves 4

sea salt
freshly ground black pepper
a few sprigs of fresh parsley

TRIM ANY SANDY STEMS OFF THE MUSH-rooms. Squeeze the lemons, then pour one-third of the juice into a bowl of cold water. Wash the mushrooms in the acidulated water. Dry them well with paper towels or a clean dish towel, then slice them thinly straight into a salad bowl.

Stir in the remaining lemon juice, then trickle in the olive oil and stir until the mushroom slices are well coated. Season to taste with salt and freshly ground black pepper. Leave to stand in a cool place for a couple of hours. Before serving, finely chop the parsley and stir into the salad.

CONCOMBRES À LA CRÈME
Creamy Cucumber Salad

DEGORGING IS ONE of the great differences between French and Anglo-Saxon approaches. Generally speaking, the French always sprinkle cucumber flesh with salt, press it down with a weighted plate and let it 'sweat' its excess moisture and bitter juices for half an hour. The texture and flavour will be distinctly finer.

2 cucumbers
coarse kosher salt
a few sprigs of fresh tarragon

Serves 4

1 lemon
150 ml single cream
freshly ground black pepper

WASH AND DRY (BUT DON'T PEEL) THE cucumbers. Run the prongs of a fork down the whole surface of each cucumber, then slice as thinly as you can, preferably with a mandolin or, alternatively, with a very sharp knife. Transfer the slices to a large strainer or colander and sprinkle with coarse salt. Place a plate or saucer on top of the cucumber slices and put a weight on it. Leave to stand for about 30 minutes.

Rinse the cucumbers thoroughly under cold running water. Pat dry with paper towels or a clean dish towel. Transfer the cucumber slices to a bowl. Snip the tarragon leaves into the bowl. Squeeze the lemon, then pour in the juice and mix well. Gradually spoon in the cream, mixing it well into the salad. Season lightly with freshly ground black pepper and refrigerate for at least 1 hour before serving.

CÉLERI RÉMOULADE
Celery Root Mayonnaise

A CREAMY-CRUNCHY traditional starter. *Sauce rémoulade* is a mayonnaise variation that is strong on mustard and normally includes capers, gherkins and sometimes anchovy. I am not alone in leaving the last three powerful ingredients out of this recipe, but they are great with cold cuts and potatoes.

Serves 4

1 to 2 celeriac roots, about
   450 g total weight
1 lemon
salt

FOR THE SAUCE *RÉMOULADE*
1 egg yolk
2 tablespoons strong Dijon
   mustard
1 teaspoon white wine vinegar
250 ml peanut oil
sea salt
freshly ground black pepper
a few sprigs of fresh parsley,
   tarragon and chervil
paprika

PEEL AND GRATE THE CELERY ROOTS, then squeeze the juice of the lemon over them and blanch in boiling salted water for a few minutes. Drain well in a large strainer or colander, squeeze out the excess moisture with your hands and leave to cool.

Meanwhile, prepare the sauce. Mix together in a bowl the egg yolk, mustard and wine vinegar until well combined. Trickle in the oil, a few drops at a time to start, whisking vigorously until you have a thick mayonnaise – see page 13. Season with salt and freshly ground black pepper.

If the mayonnaise seems too solid, whisk in 1 tablespoon of boiling water. Finely snip the fresh herbs and stir into the sauce. Chill until ready to use.

Transfer the celery roots to a serving bowl and stir in the dressing, a spoonful at a time – the celery roots should be evenly coated. Leave to chill in the refrigerator for 1 hour at the very least, giving the salad an occasional stir.

Check the dressing before serving. Sprinkle with a little paprika and extra snipped herbs.

SALADE DE TOMATES
Tomato Salad

THIS IS THE simplest of starters, and one of the best, if – and that's a pretty hefty 'if' – it is made with the right tomatoes. The right tomatoes are fragrant and firm-fleshed, juicy but not watery and ripe but not mushy. The size doesn't matter all that much, but I am suspicious of many giants, particularly on supermarket shelves. Make a note of the recipe and save for a sunny day and the perfect tomatoes.

450 g 'proper' tomatoes
2 shallots or ½ large white
　onion, if preferred
several sprigs of fresh parsley
　and chives or tarragon
4 tablespoons strong-flavoured
　olive oil

Serves 4

2 teaspoons white wine vinegar
sea salt
freshly ground black pepper

TO SERVE
fresh bread
black olives

SLICE THE TOMATOES REASONABLY THINLY and remove the core, seeds and a little of the pulp. Arrange in concentric circles on a round platter, working towards the centre.

Thinly slice the shallots or onion and scatter the rings or half-rings over the tomatoes. Snip the parsley and chives or tarragon and then scatter over the dish.

Whisk together the olive oil and vinegar, then season with sea salt and a little black pepper. Sprinkle the dressing over the salad as evenly as possible. Leave to stand for 15 minutes or so before you eat – it will taste infinitely better at room temperature. Mop up the juices with plenty of fresh bread and have a bowl of black olives on the table.

Tapenade
Black Olive Purée

A RELAXING APÉRITIF is the best prelude to an enjoyable meal. And no proper apéritif is complete without some homemade *amuse-gueule*, a tasty little 'palate-tickler' that will keep everybody happy even if they have to wait for a late fellow-guest or a problematic dish. *Tapenade* served with croutons is a summer favourite and much to be recommended with a glass of flinty cold Provence rosé, or pastis, if you prefer.

120 g fleshy black olives,
  stoned
1 or 2 cloves of garlic
a little fresh thyme, summer
  savoury and coriander leaf

Serves 4

strong-flavoured olive oil
1 small anchovy fillet in oil
  (optional)
freshly ground black pepper

CHOP UP THE OLIVES AND CRUSH THE garlic. Discard the stems from the fresh herbs and shred the leaves. Pound together the olives, garlic and herbs, using a mortar and pestle, gradually adding olive oil until you have a thick, smoothish paste.

Cut up and mash the anchovy fillet, if using, then work it into the paste, adding more olive oil. Taste and season with freshly ground black pepper. Alternatively, whizz all the ingredients together in the food processor – check the taste before seasoning.

Anchoïade
Anchovy Purée

ANCHOÏADE CAN BE served cold with crudités, or hot, spread over bread and toasted. There are many versions of this dish from Provence. My old favourite family recipe comes, I believe, from Draguignan.

225 g salted anchovies, or
  120 g canned anchovy fillets
  in oil
2 to 4 cloves of garlic
1 tablespoon white wine
  vinegar

Serves 4

1 small hard-boiled egg
¼ large white onion
250 ml olive oil
thick slices of bread, to serve
freshly ground black pepper

IF YOU ARE USING SALTED ANCHOVIES, rinse them well under cold running water, then soak in fresh cold water for at least 1 hour, changing the water a couple of times. If using canned anchovies, drain off the oil.

Combine the anchovies with the garlic, vinegar, hard-boiled egg and onion in the food processor, then gradually work in three-quarters of the olive oil. If you are not using a food processor, chop up the anchovies and garlic very finely and combine with the vinegar. Chop up the egg and onion very finely too, and stir into the anchovy mixture until well combined. Beat in the olive oil a little at a time.

Spread the anchovy purée over thick slices of bread. Sprinkle on the remaining olive oil and season liberally with black pepper. Pop under the grill for a few minutes and serve hot.

Rillettes de Saumon
Salmon Rillettes

Traditional salmon rillettes are made with a mixture of cooked and smoked salmon. I prefer this version, which I often serve on buttered light rye bread with drinks before we sit down to the main course.

about 450 g good smoked
    salmon offcuts, trimmed and
    snipped into small pieces
tiny leaves from a few sprigs of
    thyme or 1 teaspoon dried
    thyme

Serves 6 to 8

juice and finely grated zest
    of 1 small unwaxed lemon
30 g soft unsalted butter
85 g plain Boursin cheese

¼ teaspoon paprika
cayenne pepper
freshly ground black pepper
sea salt
thinly sliced, buttered, light rye
    bread and a handful of
    watercress leaves, to serve

In a food processor, briefly whiz the pieces of smoked salmon with the thyme and lemon juice and zest. Scrape down the sides of the bowl, then add the butter and Boursin. Season lightly with the paprika, a touch of cayenne and black pepper. Whiz again briefly until the mixture is combined, but still a little rough. Taste and adjust the seasoning – salt, pepper or paprika. Chill for at least 20 minutes, longer if convenient. Remove from the refrigerator at least 10 minutes before serving.

Serve with or on slices of buttered rye bread, with a few watercress leaves.

Œufs Mimosa
Hard-Boiled Eggs with Anchovy Mayonnaise

A colourful starter that looks good on a buffet or party platter. Very retro!

4 large eggs
90 ml well-seasoned
    mayonnaise (see page 13)
a few sprigs of parsley

Serves 4

2 ripe tomatoes

1 cos lettuce
2 teaspoons anchovy essence
2 anchovy fillets in oil
freshly ground black pepper

Boil the eggs for 10 minutes or so, then immerse in cold water until cool enough to shell. Meanwhile, prepare the mayonnaise (see page 13) and the other ingredients. Finely snip the parsley and slice the tomatoes, discarding the seeds and whitish cores – you'll need 8 slices. Tear out, rinse and pat dry 8 to 10 presentable lettuce leaves.

Shell the hard-boiled eggs and halve them lengthways. Carefully remove the yolks with a teaspoon; reserve 2 yolks. Mash the other yolks with the anchovy essence (use a fork), then combine with half the snipped parsley and the mayonnaise. Spoon the egg and mayonnaise into the halved egg white cases. Trim the bottom of any that look wobbly.

Arrange the lettuce leaves and tomato slices on a platter, then place a stuffed half-egg on each tomato slice. Cut each anchovy fillet into 2 strips and place over each egg in a cross. Grate the reserved egg yolks over the dish – this is the mimosa effect. Sprinkle with the remaining parsley and a little black pepper. Refrigerate until ready to serve.

Melons Rafraîchis au Vin Doux
Chilled Melons with Sweet Wine

JUST LIKE PEARS and Camembert, melons are quite unpredictable. You can make sure you select a ripe melon by choosing a fruit with a good heavy feel to it. It should also give a little around the stem and at the opposite end. And if it is a Charentais or Cavaillon melon, it should also have a fruity fragrance. Infuriatingly, not every carefully chosen melon delivers. For informal meals, I always taste a silver of each melon and make sure every plate has a wedge of the day's glorious best and disappointing worst – no favouritism. For grander occasions, I go back to the old family special below. I have been delighted to notice that it seemed to be a popular summer dish in Anjou and Touraine restaurants – with the flesh carefully pressed into melon balls, of course, but that's definitely not a trick *maison*.

Serves 4

2 x 450-g promising Charentais
    or Cavaillon melons, or 4
    smaller Ogen melons
½ bottle chilled sweet white
    wine, such as Coteaux du
    Layon, Vouvray doux or
    Beaumes de Venise
freshly ground black pepper, if
    wished

HALVE THE MELONS AND SCOOP OUT THE seeds and any membranes. If you are using small Ogen melons, remove the stalk ends. Trim the bottoms if necessary so the melon 'cups' stand upright. Refrigerate for at least 40 minutes.

To serve, pour a little chilled wine into each cup – the equivalent of a small glass. Float an ice cube or two on top and serve at once. For a special finishing touch, try it also with a little sprinkling of black pepper around the rim of each melon cup.

Macédoine de Légumes Frais à la Mayonnaise

Fresh Vegetable Medley with Mayonnaise

A SUBSTANTIAL STARTER, popular with people who prefer their vegetables cooked. Add hard-boiled eggs and leftover strips of meat, fish and shellfish and you have *salade Russe*. Both dishes are pleasing when homemade, but best avoided in unknown commercial establishments. Canned *macédoine* is simply poor convenience food. I used to wonder what, if anything, Alexander the Great of Macedonia had to do with this particular dish. (Is he not linked with another dish, the early form of sorbet he fatally consumed during a long banquet after battle?) The answer was somewhat far-fetched. The *Petit Robert* dictionary, in a moment of levity, explains that *macédoine* is a light-hearted reference to the fact that Macedonia was once inhabited by a medley of people . . .

300 g carrots	Serves 4	1 tablespoon olive oil
300 g baby turnips		freshly ground black pepper
225 g green beans		150 ml mayonnaise thinned
400 g baby peas, or 225 g		down with 1 tablespoon
frozen *petits pois*		water
225 g new potatoes		a few sprigs of fresh parsley,
sea salt		tarragon, chives and chervil
½ lemon		

BRING A LARGE SAUCEPAN OF WATER TO the boil and start preparing the vegetables. Peel the carrots and baby turnips, then dice into small 0.5-cm cubes. Top and tail the beans, then slice them into small 0.5-cm segments; shell the peas; then scrape and dice the new potatoes.

Add 2 teaspoons of salt to the boiling water. Throw in the carrots and turnips and bring back to the boil. Add the beans, peas and potatoes. If using frozen *petits pois*, don't add them until the water has come back to the boil the second time. Boil for 5 to 10 minutes more, or until all the vegetables are cooked, but not too soft. Drain well and transfer to a dish. Squeeze the lemon and sprinkle the juice and olive oil over the vegetables, then season lightly with a little salt and freshly ground black pepper.

Leave until completely cool, then gently stir in the mayonnaise and snip the fresh herbs over the dish. This dish will keep in the refrigerator for a day or two.

Chou en Salade
Shredded Cabbage Salad

This was a favourite salad starter when I was a schoolgirl, ravenous but worried about my weight. I used to wolf down platefuls of the blissful stuff. To this day I prefer it to more complex coleslaw variations. The secret lies in the shredding (long, thin strips of cabbage imbibe the vinaigrette dressing better than short, stubby pieces) and in the time spent marinating.

1 small white cabbage	**Serves 4**	90 ml peanut or olive oil
1 tablespoon white wine		sea salt
vinegar		freshly ground black pepper

Discard any blemished outer leaves. Cut the cabbage into 8 wedges and remove the core with a sharp knife. Rinse in cold water, shake well and pat dry with paper towels or a clean towel. Using a sharp knife, carefully shred the cabbage into fine strips, discarding any large ribs. Alternatively, use the shredding disc of a food processor.

Transfer the shredded cabbage to a salad bowl and stir in the vinegar. Pour in the oil, stir to coat and season to taste with salt and freshly ground black pepper. Chill for a couple of hours, giving the salad a good stir once or twice.

Check the taste of the dressing before serving and add a little salt, pepper or oil as necessary. The salad tastes best when generously coated with a strong dressing.

Carottes Râpées
Grated Carrot Salad

My favourite way to ingest this vitamin-laden vegetable. The sweetness of the carrots makes this salad very appealing to veg-resistant children. Best made with mature organic carrots.

400 g carrots	**Serves 4**	75 ml olive oil
1 lemon		sea salt
1 hard-boiled egg		freshly ground black pepper
120 g stoned black olives		a few sprigs of fresh parlsey

Peel and grate each of the carrots. Transfer to a salad bowl. Squeeze the lemon, add the strained juice and toss the carrots to coat well. Grate in the hard-boiled egg, then stir in the black olives. Add the olive oil, toss well and season lightly with salt and freshly ground black pepper. Refrigerate for at least 1 hour. Remove from the refrigerator 20 minutes or so before serving. Check the seasoning and add a little extra oil, salt or pepper if necessary. Snip and stir in the parsley at the last minute.

ENTRÉES CHAUDES
Hot Appetisers

LET ME BE FRANK about this. Several of the recipes in this section are at least as fiddly and time-consuming to prepare as main fish or meat courses. Don't let this put you off. There are a number of delectable, old-fashioned classics waiting to make a comeback in the next 20-odd pages, from *tarte à l'oignon* to *gougère, escargots au Riesling* to *crêpes farcies*.

The solution is to regard them rather as the French are doing – as first courses for special occasions or as *plats uniques*, low on fish and meat, but perfectly satisfying in every other respect, when things are more casual and meals one or two courses shorter.

I think of these *entrées chaudes* as hot (or warm) snacks, some grander than others, of course, but all very relaxed, *très sympathiques* and maybe a little tentative. The French don't really have a word for snack. The nearest to it is *casse-croûte*, which means to break the crust. *Entrées chaudes* are more elaborate, but they do break the edge of your appetite. You tend to eat them while you are hungry. Perhaps this is why they are so enjoyable: the best dish may be yet to come, during this meal or some future, more structured occasion, but who cares just now.

CRÊPES FARCIES AUX EPINARDS
Pancakes Stuffed with Spinach

BRING BACK OLD-FASHIONED savoury crepes! They are fun to make, good-natured enough to keep overnight and they take kindly to leftovers. The rather beery batter below was adapted *en famille* a long time ago from a totally beery Raymond Oliver recipe that had only a little milk to melt the butter in. Vary the blend to suit your taste – there are no hard-and-fast rules.
The ham, shallot and mushroom mixture I suggested as a soufflé alternative (see page 47) also works well as a pancake filling. So does a little leftover cold chicken, briefly sautéed with snipped tarragon leaves, then stirred into the béchamel. Add a little double cream and leave out the Gruyère cheese.

175 g flour
sea salt
3 eggs
60 g butter, plus extra for the filling and to finish
175 ml milk
175 ml beer
oil for greasing
FOR THE FILLING

Makes about 15 pancakes

450 g cooked and drained spinach, or 1.5 kg fresh spinach
350 ml thick béchamel (see page 13)
120 g Gruyère cheese
sea salt
freshly ground black pepper
grated nutmeg

SIFT THE FLOUR AND SALT INTO A BOWL and make a well. Beat the eggs as for an omelette and melt the butter with a little of the milk. Using a small whisk, gently stir together the flour and eggs, then gradually pour in the milk and beer. Stir lightly until the batter is smooth and just thick enough to coat your finger. Add the melted butter and stir a little longer. Strain through a fine strainer or *chinois* and preferably leave to stand for a couple of hours.

To cook the pancakes, very lightly grease a smooth, heavy-based frying pan. I use a wad of paper towels dipped in a little oil. Heat the pan until very hot and ladle in just enough batter to cover the bottom thinly – tip the pan to spread it evenly. Cook over a medium-high heat until the underside is golden. Turn over with a spatula and cook the other side. The first pancake sometimes sticks a little, but it tends to become easier as it gets going. If your first pancake looks a little dry, whisk a little more melted butter into the batter; if it is thin and tears easily, sift in a little flour and whisk in briskly. Re-grease the pan if necessary. Allow 2 to 3 minutes for each pancake. Once cooked, stack on a plate and cover with foil until ready to use (the pancakes will keep overnight in the refrigerator).

Heat the oven to 200°C/Gas 6. Prepare the filling. If using fresh spinach, trim, rinse and blanch in boiling water. Drain well in a colander, pressing hard to get rid of excess moisture; chop finely. Sweat the chopped spinach in a little butter. Stir into the béchamel. Grate the Gruyère and stir half into the spinach sauce. Season with a little salt, a generous amount of black pepper and a good pinch of nutmeg.

Butter a baking dish. Spoon some filling over each pancake. Roll up and place in the dish. Sprinkle the pancakes with the remaining Gruyère, dot with butter and bake for 10 to 15 minutes, until hot and golden brown. Serve at once.

ŒUFS BROUILLÉS PLM
Scrambled Eggs PLM

THE FIRST DISH my father taught me to cook and a perennial family treat. Sometimes this was pure comfort food to cheer ourselves up in a still-cold house after the drive from Paris. The cupboards may have been empty, but we never arrived without a dozen eggs, a salad and some bread. Herbs were usually to be found in the garden – however puny – and the *beurre salé* kept well in the refrigerator from one visit to the next. When PLM (my father's initials) was in charge of the menu he often gave them to his guests as a starter, but the tradition has continued; when in doubt we have scrambled eggs for supper.

6 large eggs at room
  temperature
sea salt
freshly ground black pepper
butter

Serves 2 or 3

sprigs of fresh herbs –
  tarragon, chives, parsley or
  chervil, as liked
toast or crusty bread, to serve

IN A BOWL, WHISK 5 EGGS BRISKLY, BUT without letting them become fluffy. Season with salt and freshly ground black pepper. Melt a good knob of butter in a heavy-based saucepan over a very gentle heat. Tilt the pan to coat its sides with butter.

Pour in the eggs and cook gently. Stir frequently with a wooden spoon and keep the heat very low – this is not a dish you can abandon to have a chat on the phone, but you can snip the fresh herbs finely while keeping an eye on the egg mixture. When the eggs begin to look set and cooked, add the remaining egg. Stir it in well, remove from the heat and add the snipped herbs with, if you like, a little extra butter.

Adjust the seasoning. Serve at once, with toast or crusty bread. Immerse the pan in very hot water immediately – this will save a lot of effort later.

ŒUFS GRATINÉS
Gratin of Eggs and Gruyère

A CREAMY, HOT egg starter that slips down a treat.

butter
150 g Gruyère or strong
  mature Cheddar cheese
4 large eggs

Serves 4

90 ml double cream
sea salt
freshly ground black pepper

HEAT THE OVEN TO 170°C/GAS 3. Generously butter a medium-size gratin dish or 4 small ovenproof ramekins. Grate the cheese, then spread a good layer over the bottom of the dish or dishes, reserving about one-third for the topping. Carefully break the eggs over the grated cheese.

Spoon 1 tablespoon of cream over each egg and season well with salt and freshly ground black pepper. Sprinkle the remaining grated cheese over the eggs with the remaining cream. Dot with butter and cook in the oven for about 15 minutes, until golden. Serve very hot.

ŒUFS BROUILLÉS À LA TOURANGELLE
Scrambled Eggs with Rillettes

RILLETTES ARE A SPECIALTY of Touraine. They are made from pieces of pork, or goose, slowly cooked in fat in a large cauldron until molten to a soft, fatty pâté – definitely a bit of an acquired taste, but detours are made by addicts of *rillettes* to find a *charcutier* who prepares them properly. They are a traditional local starter or snack, served with chunks of bread and a glass of cool Vouvray. Packed in little waxed pots, they will keep chilled for up to three weeks – well worth bringing back from France if you become addicted.

They are particularly good combined with scrambled eggs. And so are salmon *rillettes*, a satisfying combination of fresh and smoked salmon, spices, lemon juice and butter – not from Touraine, but now appearing on delicatessen counters everywhere.

90 g *rillettes* of duck, pork, salmon or tuna 6 large eggs freshly ground black pepper	Serves 2 or 3	1 tablespoon *crème fraîche* a few sprigs of parsley toast, to serve

MELT HALF THE *RILLETTES* IN A HEAVY-based saucepan over a very low heat. Tilt the pan around until its sides are evenly coated with fat.

In a bowl, whisk 5 of the eggs and season the mixture generously with freshly ground black pepper – the *rillettes* are fairly salty so there is no need to add salt.

Pour the eggs into the pan and cook patiently, keeping the heat low and stirring frequently with a wooden spoon, until they are almost set. Stir in the remaining egg and *rillettes*, then the *crème fraîche*. Remove from the heat. Snip a little parsley over the scrambled eggs and serve at once, with hot toast passed around separately.

Œufs en Meurette
Eggs in Red Wine

The Burgundian way of poaching eggs – in a strong red wine sauce. Keeping poached eggs warm is a little fiddly, so I have gone for the easier option of poaching the eggs at the last minute in simmering water with a few drops of vinegar, rather than in the red wine stock. Incidentally, the sauce is perfect with steak and monkfish.

Serves 4

4 large eggs
4 slices French bread
red wine vinegar

For the sauce
2 shallots
1 small onion
2 cloves of garlic
at least ½ bottle full-bodied red
 wine
1 sprig of thyme
1 bay leaf
1 sprig of parsley or chervil
90 g butter, plus extra to finish
 the sauce
1 tablespoon flour
sea salt
freshly ground black pepper

Prepare the sauce. Peel and halve the shallots, onion and garlic, reserving half a clove. Make up the red wine to 750 ml with water. In a saucepan, bring the wine and water to the boil with the shallots, onion, garlic, thyme, bay leaf and parsley or chervil. Boil until reduced by half.

Meanwhile, mash together 60 g butter and the flour and divide the paste into 4 small pieces. Strain the hot wine stock through a strainer into a smaller saucepan and then gradually add the butter and flour paste, whisking in the pieces one by one. Whisking all the time, simmer the sauce for 2 minutes until it has thickened. Season to taste with salt and freshly ground black pepper; and then keep hot, stirring occasionally.

Rub the bread with the cut side of the remaining garlic and fry in butter until golden brown on both sides. Keep warm.

Rinse out the first saucepan, pour in at least 1.8 litres of boiling water, add a trickle of red wine vinegar and bring back to the boil. Stir until the water swirls around, then lower the heat a little and carefully poach the eggs for 1 to 2 minutes. I find it easiest to use a ladle to lower the eggs into the simmering water and a draining spoon to lift them out. Drain the eggs on an impeccably clean, folded towel; trim with scissors if they look too messy. Arrange one egg on each of the slices of fried bread. Whisk a few small knobs of butter into the sauce to make it look glossy, spoon it over the eggs and serve.

Omelette aux Fines Herbes
Herb Omelette

This is one of the first recipes I remember watching someone cook, one of the first I wrote down and, to my shame twenty years later, one that I still can't report to have constant success with.

My mentor, Madame Boucher, used to manage 16 eggs at the same time in an incredibly heavy, huge, battered black frying pan.

Invariably her omelettes turned out moistly creamy inside, packed with specks of fragrant herbs from the garden, and golden on the outside. Accompanied by the other deceptively simple dish, *pommes de terre sautées* (see page 124), another Boucher triumph, it made a perfect dinner.

several sprigs of fresh herbs –
    tarragon or chives and
    parsley and/or chervil
4 large eggs
1 tablespoon milk

Serves 2

sea salt
freshly ground black pepper
45 g butter, plus a little extra to
    finish

Snip the herbs very finely and reserve. In a bowl, using a fork, beat the eggs briskly with 1 tablespoon of cold water and the milk for about 20 seconds. Whisk in half the snipped herbs and season to taste with salt and freshly ground black pepper.

Meanwhile, heat a smallish, heavy-based frying pan until it is very hot. Add 30 g butter and swirl it around to coat the pan. Before the butter starts browning, pour in the beaten eggs. Reduce the heat a little. Cook the omelette, shaking the pan to prevent the eggs from sticking. Also, occasionally stir the edges of the mixture towards the centre of the pan when it begins to set.

As soon as the eggs are no longer liquid, but still looking moist, slip the rest of the butter under the omelette and sprinkle half the remaining herbs on top. Gently tilt the handle of the pan down towards you and fold the omelette back towards the centre with the help of a metal spatula. Now lift up the handle of the pan away from you and turn the omelette upside down on to a heated plate. Trail a little extra butter over the omelette, sprinkle with the rest of the *fines herbes* and serve.

PIPÉRADE

Tomato and Sweet Pepper Omelette

My SUCCESS RATE with large folded omelettes being more than erratic, I have long been a fan of *pipérade*, the celebrated sweet pepper and egg dish from the Basque country. It looks appetising, requires no folding and is a good dish to serve when you haven't got a great deal of time at the finish. Prepare the vegetable purée ahead and reheat it while you are whisking the eggs. Serve with Bayonne ham, bread and a green salad for an easy supper or brunch.

1 large red pepper
1 onion
olive oil or bacon fat
3 cloves of garlic
3 or 4 ripe tomatoes
a pinch of dried thyme
1 bay leaf

Serves 4

2 slices Bayonne or similar
   cured ham
a little sweet vermouth or
   1 teaspoon sugar
sea salt
freshly ground black pepper
8 large eggs

WASH AND DRY THE PEPPER, THEN CUT IT in half and remove the seeds, core and membrane. Char under the grill, uncut side up, until the skin is blistered. When the pepper is cool enough to handle, remove the skin and cut the flesh into small strips.

Chop the onion. In a large sauté pan or frying pan, heat a little olive oil or bacon fat and cook the onion with the whole garlic cloves, keeping the heat low. Blanch the tomatoes, then remove the skins and seeds and chop up the flesh. Add with the pepper, thyme and bay leaf to the onion and cook for about 15 minutes, stirring occasionally, until you have a thickish, chunky purée.

Chop the ham into pieces and add to the purée, with a sprinkling of sweet vermouth or 1 teaspoon of sugar to take away any

acidity. Season to taste with salt and freshly ground black pepper. Remove the garlic cloves and bay leaf. A few minutes before serving, reheat the pepper mixture.

Break 4 eggs into each of 2 bowls and beat briskly with a fork. Divide the pepper mixture between the 2 bowls and combine well with the beaten eggs. Grease 2 medium frying pans with olive oil and heat both pans and the grill. When the pans are hot, pour in the mixture and cook for a few minutes over a low heat, stirring frequently, until the bottom of the *pipérade* is set.

Finish off under the grill for a couple of minutes, until lightly set and just coloured. I find it easier to produce a *pipérade* using 2 small frying pans, but you might prefer to cook it in a single batch. Serve at once.

Soufflé au Gruyère
Cheese Soufflé

NOT EXACTLY AN original dish, I know, but one that is hard to beat and never fails to bring pleasure to the palate.

250 ml milk
1 bay leaf
sea salt
freshly ground black pepper
90 g butter, plus extra for
  greasing
75 g flour

Serves 4 to 6

5 eggs
1 teaspoon strong Dijon
  mustard
grated nutmeg
120 g Gruyère or other strong
  hard cheese

BRING THE MILK TO THE BOIL WITH THE BAY leaf, a pinch of salt and a little black pepper; take off the heat. Melt the butter, add the flour and cook gently for a couple of minutes, stirring constantly with a whisk. Pour in the hot milk, whisking briskly and bring to the boil. Reduce the heat and simmer until the sauce is smooth and thick, stirring frequently. Remove from the heat.

Separate the eggs, then whisk the yolks into the sauce. Season with a little salt and pepper, the mustard and a pinch of nutmeg.

Grate in the Gruyère. The mixture can be set aside for a while at this stage.

Heat the oven to 190°C/Gas 5 and generously butter a 20-cm soufflé dish. Whisk the egg whites until stiff. Using a large metal spoon, gently fold a little whisked egg white into the sauce. Fold in the rest thoroughly, working lightly and upwards, to keep in as much air as possible. Pour into the prepared soufflé dish, level with a spatula and bake for 25 to 35 minutes, until brown and well risen. Serve at once.

Escargots au Riesling
Snails with Wine Sauce

A very good way of serving snails if you don't happen to have the necessary equipment to extract them from their shells. You can, of course, start from scratch, with live snails, in which case this is a real plan-ahead recipe, as you have to starve them for a week before you start cooking. I know I am too feeble-hearted to last the course and likely to let the snails loose in the dead of night, so I use good-quality canned *escargots* in London and freshly cooked ones from the *charcuterie* in France.

If you are disappointed not to see a proper snail butter recipe at this stage, turn to *moules farcies* (page 63) or *champignons farcis* (page 130). I love *buerre d'escargot* best of all with mushrooms and second best with mussels, but somehow not with snails.

Serves 4

2 shallots
2 cloves of garlic
a small bunch of fresh parsley
60 g butter, plus extra for the
    toast
24 to 30 snails, canned and
    drained, or freshly cooked
8 slices French bread
100 ml Alsace Riesling
2 teaspoons flour
120 ml *crème fraîche*
sea salt
freshly ground black pepper

Finely chop the shallots, 1 clove of garlic and the parsley. Melt the butter in a sauté pan. Add the chopped shallots and garlic and half the parsley. Stir for a few minutes over a gentle heat. Add the snails and sauté for 2 to 3 minutes, stirring occasionally.

Meanwhile, prepare the toast. Cut the remaining clove of garlic in half. Rub the bread with the cut sides of the garlic, then butter lightly. Heat the grill.

Pour the wine into the snail mixture and bring to a simmer. Sprinkle the flour over the mixture, stir and cook for 5 to 10 minutes. Then stir in the *crème fraîche* and heat through gently. Toast the bread under the grill.

Season the snails generously with sea salt and freshly ground black pepper.

As a finishing touch, gently sprinkle the remaining parsley over the snails and serve at once with the hot toast.

CROÛTES AU FROMAGE
Hot Cheese Croustades

A DISH I WELL REMEMBER circulating with at parties in my role of eldest daughter and *jeune fille de la maison*. French country bread, *pain de campagne*, was what we used. Monsieur Poilâne's bread is ideal if you are lucky enough to be able to find it. Try serving with a mixed leaf salad as a change from the ubiquitous goat cheese starter.

6 slices mixed-grain bread,
  medium cut
60 g butter
200 g Gruyère or similar
  strongly flavoured hard
  cheese

Serves 4

2 small eggs
2 tablespoons *crème fraîche* or
  sour cream
grated nutmeg
freshly ground black pepper
a few sprigs of chives

HEAT THE GRILL. IF YOU PREFER, REMOVE the crusts from the bread. Butter on one side. The slices can be left whole, halved or quartered – the smaller the better if you are serving them as finger food. Grate the cheese into a bowl and mix with the eggs and *crème fraîche*. Season to taste with nutmeg and freshly ground black pepper. Generously spread the cheese mixture over the bread. Arrange in a flameproof dish and grill for a few minutes until golden brown.

Meanwhile, finely snip the chives. Serve hot or *tiède*, sprinkled with snipped chives and a little extra black pepper.

CROQUE-MONSIEUR MAISON
Toasted Cheese and Ham

WHEN IN DOUBT, when you can't face the thought of cooking and can't think of anything to cook anyway, give them a *croque-monsieur*. Always in great demand from junior members of the family and not exactly frowned on by their seniors, the archetypal French café snack is wonderful emergency food.

3 tablespoons olive oil
8 slices of bread
60 to 90 g butter
120 g Gruyère or Cheddar
  cheese

Serves 4

4 thick slices good cooked ham
  off the bone
2 to 3 teaspoons Dijon mustard
a few sprigs of chives

HEAT THE GRILL. IN A LARGE FRYING PAN, heat the olive oil and brown one side of each slice of bread. Remove from the pan and butter the uncooked sides. Grate the cheese and spread over 4 slices, on the buttered sides. Heat under the grill until melting.

Divide the ham between the remaining buttered pieces of bread, if necessary, trimming the ham slices to fit. Spread some mustard over the ham. Snip the chives and sprinkle them over the ham.

Melt the remaining butter in the frying pan. Heat the ham-covered slices of bread in the hot butter, fried sides down. Sandwich with the toasted cheese slices, cheese side down. Press well together and eat very hot.

Feuilleté au Roquefort
Roquefort Cheese Puff

A MORE PROPER name for this recipe would be *demi-feuilleté au Roquefort*, since the pastry is very much a shortcut on traditional puff. The filling is rich and festive.

FOR THE PASTRY
225 g flour
pinch of salt
90 ml double cream
120 g butter, plus extra for
  greasing
1 egg yolk and a little milk, for
  glazing

Serves 6 to 8

FOR THE FILLING
4 eggs
150 g Roquefort cheese
90 g cream cheese
90 ml single cream
freshly ground black pepper
a small bunch of fresh chives

TO MAKE THE PASTRY BY HAND, SIFT THE flour and salt into a bowl. Make a well and add the cream. Lightly work the flour into the cream, adding a couple of tablespoons of very cold water if the flour isn't completely absorbed. Cut the butter into small pieces, add half to the flour and knead gently until absorbed, working the pastry as little as possible. Divide the pastry into 4 pieces, mix a bit of butter into each piece, then roll together to form a large ball.

If you are using a food processor, cut the butter into very small pieces. Briefly process the flour and salt. Add half the butter and process until the mixture resembles breadcrumbs. With the machine still running, add the cream and 1 tablespoon of cold water until the dough starts to form a ball and comes off the sides of the bowl. Add the remaining butter, dotting over the dough and process just enough to mix it well in.

Whichever method you have used, once you have a ball of dough, turn it out on to a floured board, then flatten lightly with a floured rolling pin and fold and roll a couple of times. Chill the folded pastry for at least 30 minutes (but no longer than 1 hour, otherwise it hardens too much) before using.

Meanwhile, prepare the filling. Whisk the 4 eggs. In another bowl, mash the Roquefort with a fork. Combine the Roquefort, cream cheese and cream, whisking the mixture until fairly smooth. Add the eggs and whisk well. Season generously with freshly ground black pepper and snip in the chives.

Heat the oven to 190°C/Gas 5. Separate the pastry into 2 pieces, with one 'half' slightly larger than the other. Roll out into circles. Grease a large, flan tin and spread the smaller pastry circle on it. Prick well with a fork. Spoon the filling over the pastry.

Cover with the remaining pastry. Insert a pastry funnel in the centre to allow the steam to escape. Seal the edges by lightly pressing together with dampened fingers. Score the top in a diamond pattern with a knife. Glaze the pastry with beaten egg yolk and a little milk. Bake for 40 to 45 minutes.

Gougère

Cheese Choux Ring

As satisfying to make as to eat, particularly with a good glass of wine. This recipe is for a *gougère* ring. To make individual puffs, keep the paste balls at least 2.5 cm apart when you pipe or spoon them on to the baking tray.

120 g butter, plus extra for greasing 150 g flour 250 ml water salt	Serves 6	3 or 4 eggs 120 g Emmental, Comté or mature farmhouse Cheddar freshly ground black pepper dash of milk, for glazing

Cut the butter into dice. Sift the flour on to a sheet of greaseproof paper. In a heavy-based saucepan, bring the water, diced butter and a pinch of salt to the boil. The minute the liquid begins to boil, remove the pan from the heat. Quickly and all at once add the flour and immediately start stirring it in with a spatula or wooden spoon. Return to the heat and continue to stir briskly until the paste leaves the sides of the pan and looks smooth and a little shiny.

Remove from the heat and then stir for 1 minute. Add the eggs, one at a time, mixing them in vigorously until the paste comes together again. Beat the last egg before you add it in, since you may need only a fraction of it: you should end up with a glossy, floppy paste, not a runny, liquid one. Continue beating for another minute or

so to give the paste more body. Cut the cheese into slivers and beat into the paste. Season with freshly ground black pepper.

Heat the oven to 190°C/Gas 5. Grease a baking tray. Fit a pastry bag with a plain 1-cm tip and spoon the paste into the bag. Pipe a large ring of small balls of paste on the baking tray, keeping them no farther than 2 cm apart. If you don't like using a piping bag, you can use a tablespoon – the final effect will not be quite so tidy, but I don't see this as being a problem. Brush the paste lightly with any remaining egg yolk mixed with a splash of milk.

Bake for about 30 minutes, until well risen and golden. Turn the oven off (and open the door if electric). Leave the *gougère* to stand for 5 minutes before taking it out. Serve hot or warm.

Petites Bouchées
Savoury Puffs

A *bouchée* is a mouthful and I have always thought of these soft-centered little morsels as excellent 'mouth-fillers'. They certainly give the hostess or host time to control the subject of the conversation while guests are palatably occupied.

If you are getting out your pastry bag to make neat choux puffs, try piping some of the paste into small éclairs for contrast. These *bouchées* are good cold, but don't assemble them more than 1 to 2 hours ahead. Unfilled baked puffs or éclairs will freeze well, otherwise use them on the day you make them.

Serves 6

FOR THE CHOUX PUFFS
120 g butter, plus extra for greasing
150 g flour
250 ml water
salt
3 or 4 eggs
freshly ground black pepper
300 ml thick béchamel (see page 13)

FOR THE PRAWN FILLING
90 g small cooked peeled prawns
30 ml double cream
cayenne pepper
a few sprigs of chives

FOR THE MUSHROOM FILLING
30 g butter
175 g brown cap mushrooms
1 clove of garlic
2 teaspoons tomato purée
a few sprigs of parsley

FOR THE BLUE CHEESE FILLING
90 g Fourme d'Ambert or similar blue cheese
1 stick of celery
2 tablespoons double cream
paprika

HEAT THE OVEN TO 190°C/GAS 5. MAKE the choux paste (see page 51) and pipe or spoon on to a greased baking tray, keeping the paste balls at least 2.5 cm apart. Bake for about 30 minutes, until well risen and golden; leave to cool.

Meanwhile, prepare the fillings. To make the prawn filling, press the prawns dry between 2 sheets of paper towels, then cut in half. In a bowl, mix together one-third of the béchamel, the chopped prawns and the cream. Season with a good pinch of cayenne and a little salt. Snip in the chives.

To make the mushroom filling, melt the butter in a small frying pan. Finely chop the mushrooms and garlic, then sauté over a medium heat. In a bowl, combine one-third of the béchamel with the tomato purée. Stir in the sautéed mushrooms and snip in the parsley. Season with salt and black pepper.

For the blue cheese filling, mash the cheese with a fork. Finely chop the celery. Mix with the remaining béchamel and the cream. Season with a good pinch of paprika.

Slit the puffs with a knife. Spoon the prawn filling into one-third of the puffs, then the mushroom filling into another third and the blue cheese filling into the rest.

Tarte à l'Oignon
Onion Tart

A VERY ONIONY onion tart. The evaporated milk adds a distinctive rich sweetness to the filling. If you like a touch of *lardons* with onions, add about 90 g chopped and sautéed smoked bacon drained on paper towels to the filling.

FOR THE PASTRY
150 g cold butter, plus extra for greasing
225 g flour
pinch of salt
1 teaspoon sugar
1 egg
1 egg white

Serves 8

FOR THE FILLING
1.2 kg large white onions
2 or 3 fresh sage leaves
4 to 5 tablespoons olive oil
3 eggs

100 ml evaporated milk or single cream
30 g strong Gruyère or similar cheese
sea salt
freshly ground black pepper
grated nutmeg

PREPARE THE PASTRY CASE. CUT THE butter into small pieces. If you are using a food processor, combine the flour, salt and sugar, then add the butter and process until the mixture looks like breadcrumbs. Add the egg and 5 or 6 tablespoons of cold water. Process until the mixture comes off the sides of the bowl. Remove the pastry from the bowl, work lightly with your hands into a ball and chill for at least 30 minutes.

Alternatively, cut up the butter and leave to soften. Sift the flour into a bowl with the salt and sugar. Make a well, add the butter, the egg and 5 or 6 tablespoons of cold water. Mix with your fingertips without trying to get a smooth paste. Add a little more water if necessary – the paste should be supple but not soft. Form into a ball and chill as above.

Butter a large, loose-bottomed tart tin. Roll out the pastry, then spread it into the greased tin, using your hands to press it in lightly without stretching it. Prick with a fork and chill for 10 minutes.

Heat the oven to 200°C/Gas 6. Line the pastry case with greaseproof paper or foil and evenly fill with dried beans. Then bake the case for 15 to 20 minutes.

Meanwhile, prepare the filling. Very thinly slice the onions – it doesn't matter if the slices break. Finely snip the sage leaves. In a large frying pan, heat the olive oil, then gently sweat the onion slices with the chopped sage until soft and blond, but not too browned; keep the heat very low and the pan covered, occasionally lifting the lid to stir the onions. Allow a good 30 minutes for the onions to be really soft.

Remove the dried beans and lining paper from the pastry case. If the base still feels very soft, return the tin to the oven for a few minutes. Leave to cool a little, then brush the pastry with a little egg white. Turn the oven down to 190°C/Gas 5.

Lightly whisk together the eggs and the evaporated milk or cream. Stir into the onion mixture. Grate in the cheese. Season generously with salt and freshly ground black pepper and a little nutmeg. Pour into the prepared pastry case and bake for 15 to 20 minutes. Serve warm rather than hot.

Pissaladière
Provençal Onion and Anchovy Tart

A favourite summer dish and one that I have always thought of as 'convenience' food, because we always used fresh bread dough from the village baker for the crust. Had I been more romantic I would perhaps have been reminded of the days of communal baking.

Now that I cannot easily get hold of fresh bread dough I use store-bought puff pastry, preferably fresh, and concentrate on gently cooking the filling until the onions sweetly melt. The tomatoes do not feature in original Provençal recipes for *pissaladière*, but I like their texture.

450 g ready-made puff pastry
butter or oil for greasing
1 small egg, separated

For the filling
1 kg large white onions
4 tablespoons strong-flavoured
   olive oil

Serves 6 to 8

2 tomatoes
a few sprigs of fresh thyme
sea salt
freshly ground black pepper
1 teaspoon sugar
about 24 canned anchovy
   fillets
about 12 black olives

Prepare the filling. Thinly slice the onions. Heat the oil in a large frying pan and sauté the onions over a very low heat. Meanwhile, blanch, peel, seed and chop the tomatoes. Add the sprigs of thyme to the onions and continue to sauté over a low heat for 30 minutes, until the onions are very soft. Stir occasionally and be careful that the onions don't brown.

Heat the oven to 220°C/Gas 7. Roll out the pastry to about 0.5 cm thick. Grease a baking tray. Cut the pastry into a 25-cm square and spread it on to the sheet.

Cut the remaining pastry into 4 strips, 25 cm long and 1 cm wide. Brush the surface of each strip with egg white, then stick one strip along each side of the pastry square, brushed surface down.

Remove the sprigs of thyme from the frying pan. Season the onion and tomato filling very lightly with salt and pepper and stir in the sugar. Spoon the filling over the dough, keeping clear of the edges. Drain the anchovy fillets. Arrange attractively over the filling and dot about the black olives.

Beat the remaining egg white with the yolk and brush the edges of the pastry. Bake for 15 to 20 minutes, then lower the heat to 190°C/Gas 5 and bake for 5 to 10 minutes more, until the top is golden and the pastry base cooked – check by lifting it a little with a spatula. Eat *tiède* at room temperature.

QUICHE LORRAINE
Quiche Lorraine

CLOSE YOUR EYES and think of ten classic French dishes. I would be surprised if *quiche lorraine* did not feature somewhere on your list. You may be surprised to hear that this most famous French dish, the matriarch of the egg-and-cream filled family of tarts, derives its name from that very German word for cake – *kuchen*. The original *quiche lorraine* recipes from Nancy did not include cheese, but many people prefer it with, so I have added it as an optional extra. More important than the presence, or absence, of cheese is the quality of the bacon you use. The best bet (and a bit of a tall order) is traditionally cured, lightly smoked bacon, cut into very thick slices.

225 g cold butter, plus extra for
   greasing
375 g flour
pinch of salt

FOR THE FILLING
225 g smoked bacon, cut into
   very thick slices

Serves 6 to 8

1 to 2 tablespoons olive oil
3 large eggs
150 ml double cream or *crème
   fraîche*
freshly ground black pepper
sea salt, if you like
30 g butter
45 g Gruyère cheese (optional)

PREPARE THE PASTRY CASE. CUT THE butter into small cubes. If you are using a food processor, quickly whizz together the flour and salt. Add half the butter and process until the mixture looks like breadcrumbs. With the machine still running, add 5 or 6 tablespoons of cold water through the feed tube and process until the mixture forms a ball and comes off the sides of the bowl. Divide the ball into 4 pieces, return to the processor and add the remaining butter (dotted evenly over the dough). Process until well mixed.

Remove the dough from the bowl. On a floured board, roll it into a long rectangle (don't be too pedantic about this – rounded corners are fine) and then fold both ends towards the centre. Roll out again and repeat 3 times. Chill for at least 30 minutes.

Alternatively, sift the flour and salt into a bowl. Make a well, add 5 or 6 tablespoons of very cold water and lightly gather the flour into the water. Work the dough with your fingertips, then flatten it on a floured board.

Dot with the cubes of cold butter, press them in well and fold over 3 times crossways, like a letter, then fold 3 times lengthways. Chill for 10 minutes and then roll and fold as above 3 more times, leaving the dough to rest in the refrigerator in between the rollings.

Heat the oven to 190°C/Gas 5. Butter a large, loose-bottomed tart tin. Roll out the pastry, then spread it into the greased tin. Leave it to overhang a little from the tin. Prick all over with a fork. Line the pastry case with foil or greaseproof paper and fill with dried beans. Bake for 15 minutes, remove the beans and lining paper.

To make the filling, remove the rind from the bacon, if necessary, then cut into 0.75-cm pieces. If you suspect that the bacon is very salty, blanch it in boiling water and pat it dry with paper towels. Heat the oil and sauté the bacon until golden; drain on paper towels. Spread the bacon evenly over the pastry and press it in a little.

Beat the eggs and the cream, season with freshly ground black pepper. Pour into the pastry shell and dot with butter. If using Gruyère, grate it and sprinkle over the tart before adding the butter. Bake for 15 to 20 minutes, until set. Cover the tart with greaseproof paper if colouring quickly. Serve warm.

Tarte à la Moutarde
Mustard Tart

A ROBUST TART for mustard lovers.

Serves 6 to 8

1 pastry case, half-baked (see *tarte à l'oignon* on page 53)

FOR THE FILLING
150 g Gruyère or similar strong cheese
2 tablespoons strong Dijon mustard

2 tablespoons single cream or evaporated milk
3 tomatoes
sea salt
freshly ground black pepper
dried thyme and savoury
2 tablespoons strong-flavoured olive oil

PREPARE AND BAKE THE PASTRY CASE. Heat the oven to 190°C/Gas 5. Make the filling. Grate the cheese and sprinkle one-quarter of it over the pastry. Mix the mustard with the cream or evaporated milk and pour over the grated cheese.

Blanch and peel the tomatoes. Cut into thin slices and remove the seeds. Sprinkle another quarter of the cheese over the mustard and cream mixture. Arrange the tomato slices on top. Season lightly with salt and pepper. Crumble in a pinch or two of dried herbs and cover with the remaining cheese. Sprinkle with the olive oil and black pepper, if desired.

Bake for about 20 minutes, until golden brown. Leave to cool slightly before serving to eat *tiède*.

Tarte à la Ratatouille
Mixed Vegetable Tart

A MOST DEPENDABLE COMBINATION and a civilised way of using leftover *ratatouille* (see the recipe on page 121). If you are starting from scratch, however, halve the quantities given in the recipe and leave out the parsley and final tablespoon of olive oil. Serve, like other savoury tarts, as a starter (for 6 to 8) or with a salad as a relaxed main course (for 4 to 6).

Serves 6 to 8

1 pastry case, fully baked (see page 53)

cooked ratatouille (see above)
1 or 2 ripe tomatoes

PREPARE AND BAKE THE PASTRY CASE. HEAT the oven to 190°C/Gas 5.

Chop and seed the tomatoes, then stir them into the ratatouille. Spoon the mixture into the prepared pastry case and smooth flat. Bake the tart for 10 to 15 minutes, then remove from the oven and leave to cool until barely warm before serving.

Tarte aux Epinards
Spinach Tart

Like many of its fellow savoury tarts, *tarte aux épinards* is a very easy dinner-party first course, as it is best eaten barely warm and can be dealt with before the guests arrive. It would be dishonest of me not to mention that I sometimes make this dish with 450 g frozen spinach, well drained, instead of the fresh stuff when speed is of the essence – or the market spinachless.

1 pastry case, half-baked
  (see *tarte à l'oignon* recipe on
  page 53)

For the filling
1.5 kg fresh spinach
sea salt
75 g butter

Serves 6 to 8

1 tablespoon flour
250 ml *crème fraîche*
freshly ground black pepper
4 eggs
grated nutmeg
30 g Gruyère or similar strong
  cheese

Prepare and bake the pastry case. Make the filling while the pastry case is in the oven. Trim and wash the spinach. Wilt the leaves for 1 minute in a little salted boiling water. Drain well in a colander, pushing with a wooden spoon to extract as much moisture as possible; chop roughly. Melt a knob of butter in a pan, add the chopped spinach and sweat for 1 minute. Reserve.

In a saucepan, melt the remaining butter. Add the flour and cook for 2 minutes, stirring constantly. Spoon in the *crème fraîche* and cook until thickened, stirring frequently. Season generously with salt and freshly ground black pepper; remove from the heat.

Beat the eggs thoroughly, then whisk them into the cream sauce. Fold three-quarters of this mixture into the spinach. Check the seasoning and add a little nutmeg. Pour into the half-baked pastry case. Top with the remaining cream and egg sauce. Grate the cheese and sprinkle over the tart.

Bake the tart at 190°C/Gas 5 for about 20 minutes, until firm and golden. Leave to cool before serving – this tart is best served *tiède*.

Tarte aux Tomates Toute Simple
Tomato Tart

The best tomato tart I have ever eaten was in a Paris restaurant called Chez Francis near the Pont de l'Alma. The restaurant was all weathered mirrors and red banquettes, the clientèle smooth and *très parisienne*. The tomato tart was a glorious concoction of melting tomatoes and buttery puff pastry. We have all had so much tomato doused in extra-virgin olive oil that I feel like campaigning for tomatoes anointed with butter. It brings out their sweetness. This recipe makes a perfect lunch for 4 people with a green salad or a nifty dinner party starter for 6.

Serves 4 to 6

225 g ready-made chilled puff
  pastry in a sheet
30 g butter
about 1 kg ripe fresh tomatoes
2 tablespoons sunflower or
  mild-tasting olive oil
1 teaspoon caster sugar

1 tablespoon freshly grated
  Parmesan or Gruyère cheese
1 teaspoon dried marjoram or
  oregano
a few leaves fresh basil, to
  finish
sea salt and freshly ground
  black pepper

Roll out the sheet of puff pastry. Generously butter the bottom and sides of a large, loose-bottomed tart tin. Place the pastry in the tin, fit in loosely, then use a small, sharp knife to nick in crosses and chill for at least 20 minutes.

Cut the tomatoes into thick slices (about 0.5 cm). Place on a clean towel or a double layer of paper towels. Sprinkle with salt and set aside for 15 minutes.

Heat the oil in a large frying pan over a moderate heat. Sauté the tomatoes, sprinkled with sugar, in single layers, for 5 minutes each side. Reserve in a colander and put a plate under it to collect the juices.

Heat the oven with a large baking tray inside to 200°C/Gas 6. Take the pastry out of the refrigerator and sprinkle with the grated Parmesan and herbs. Arrange the tomatoes on top in overlapping circles, starting from the outside. Season again lightly and sprinkle with 1 tablespoon of the tomato juices (the rest can be added to a sauce, soup or dressing). Dot with the reserved butter and bake for 10 to 12 minutes, until golden and bubbling. Check that the pastry is baked through after 10 minutes: if the tomatoes are browning too fast, cover loosely with lightly crushed foil.

Serve warm rather than hot, decorated with torn basil leaves.

Jambon à la Crème
Ham in Cream and Port Wine Sauce

When I moved into my first flat after leaving university, my aunt Yvonée – who was a nice combination of intellectual, *gourmande* and good cook – empathised with my situation. What could a novice cook and fledgling career girl impress her friends with? She gave me as a culinary bible her own copy of Curnonsky. She looked through her cards, books and scrapbooks and went to a great deal of trouble to write down her chosen recipes. I was quite overwhelmed, but this quick-and-easy starter soon caught my eye. It works well, followed by a large *salade niçoise*, as a quick supper – particularly if your guests turn up the minute you walk in.

Serves 4

4 thick slices of good cooked
  ham off the bone
30 g butter
mini croissants, to serve

For the sauce
90 ml port wine
90 ml tomato *coulis* (see page
  15)

90 ml sour cream or *crème
  fraîche*
sea salt
freshly ground black pepper

Jambons.Saucissons.Salaisons.Conserves.
'ALHAMBRA'

Heat the oven to 100°C/Gas low. Heat the croissants and the serving dish. In a saucepan, combine the port wine, tomato *coulis* and cream. Heat until very hot, but be careful not to boil, stirring frequently.

Meanwhile, melt the butter in a frying pan and heat the ham. Roll each slice and place in the heated serving dish. Season the sauce with salt and plenty of ground black pepper. Pour over the ham and serve with the croissants.

Poissons et Fruits de Mer
Fish and Seafood

Our local Paris street market, rue Poncelet in the XVIIth, wasn't particularly distinguished by Paris standards. Naturally it was noisy, narrow and colourful. It was also unpretentiously very well supplied. I still pay it my respects whenever I am staying in Paris. Its glorious fish and seafood displays – and choice – I still miss a great deal. Finding good seafood or fish in London is an expensive and laborious exercise, reeking of foodie snobbery.

It seems that Paris was always well supplied with fish. When Elizabeth of Austria, the new wife of King Charles IX, first arrived in Paris in 1570, the municipality decided to hold a banquet in her honour. But it was Lent and the Church kept to its rules: no meat was to be allowed. The Queen Mother's fishmongers came to the rescue. No problem. They could guarantee to supply sole, turbot, mullet, trout, carp, pike, lamprey, salmon (fresh and salted), shad, herring, lobsters, crabs, crayfish, mussels and a thousand frogs. They couldn't quite promise mackerel, sturgeon, porpoise and tortoise, but they were hopeful . . . Not a bad spread to pick from.

Langoustines
Dublin Bay Prawns

Truly a food to feast on. *Langoustines* traditionally feature on the family menu at least once sometime over Christmas and the New Year. Since every other French family tends to do just the same and prices inevitably rocket a little higher every year, this isn't a particularly bright move in terms of economics. Even apart from Christmas, *langoustines* have always been a family treat. When one member of the family wants to be nice to us all, he or she buys as many crustaceans as the cash flow permits, makes a mayonnaise and we tuck merrily in – armed with a bottle of Chablis or Alsace Pinot Gris, finger bowls, large napkins and suitable hardware to extract the last bit of flesh from the claws. Not a pretty sight for outsiders, but plenty of happy memories for the Moines.

There are elaborate ways of cooking *langoustines*, but not in my book. I think they are best either *au naturel* or simply pan-fried. Allow six *langoustines* per person, four at the very least. The heads and shells are worth keeping for making stock. A pinch of saffron is a desirable optional extra.

---

24 raw, unshelled *langoustines*
1 lemon, cut into wedges, to
    serve

LANGOUSTINES AU NATUREL
150 ml dry white wine
sea salt
2 shallots

Serves 4

1 bay leaf
90 g butter, if serving hot
150 ml mayonnaise (see page
    13), if serving cold
1 lemon

LANGOUSTINES POÊLÉES
1 tablespoon olive oil
60 g butter
1 shallot
1 clove of garlic
several sprigs of parsley
½ lemon

LANGOUSTINES AU NATUREL

In a very large saucepan, bring to the boil plenty of water, the wine, a generous pinch of salt, the shallots and the bay leaf. Simmer for a few minutes.

Wash the *langoustines* in cold water. Turn up the heat, bring the liquid back to a fast boil and add the *langoustines*. Return to the boil and cook for 3 to 5 minutes, depending on the size of the *langoustines*.

Turn off the heat and leave the *langoustines* in the stock for a few minutes; drain and refresh under cold water. Serve either hot with melted butter, or cold with mayonnaise. Serve with wedges of lemon.

LANGOUSTINES POÊLÉES

Cook the *langoustines* as before but for 2 minutes only. As soon as they are cool enough to handle, shell them. Start by twisting or cutting, off the heads. Pull the shell apart, slitting the undersides with scissors if necessary, then holding the tail shell and pulling the meat free. Remove any large dark intestinal threads, rinse and dry.

Heat the oil and butter in a large sauté pan. Chop the shallot and garlic and soften for a minute. Add the *langoustines* and sauté gently all over 2 to 3 minutes. Snip in the parsley and sprinkle with the juice of ½ lemon. Serve with pan juices and with lemon wedges.

Moules Marinière
Mussels in White Wine

A HOMEGROWN COMPROMISE: this version of *moules marinière* includes a little cream, but is not as rich as the roux-and-egg based *moules pulette*.

3 litres or 1.8 kg mussels in
  their shells
2 shallots
1 clove of garlic
60 g butter
several sprigs of parsley
a few sprigs of chives

Serves 4 to 6

a few sprigs of thyme
250 ml dry white wine
200 ml water
sea salt
freshly ground black pepper
4 tablespoons double cream
fresh crusty bread, to serve

SCRUB THE MUSSELS UNDER COLD RUNNING water and remove the black beards. Discard any of the mussels that remain open or look cracked; then keep the mussels in plenty of cold water.

Finely chop the shallots and garlic. Melt the butter in a very large saucepan, then add the chopped shallots and garlic and sweat for a couple of minutes. Snip in the parsley, chives and thyme, reserving a few sprigs to finish the dish. Pour in the white wine and water and bring to the boil. Reduce the heat and simmer the liquid for a few minutes.

Add the mussels, turn up the heat and season with very little salt and plenty of black pepper. Cook for 3 to 5 minutes, until the mussels open, shaking the pan occasionally. If any mussels have failed to open, you must discard them. Remove the mussels with a draining spoon and heap them in a large bowl.

Increase the heat a little, add the cream to the pan and stir in well. Pour the sauce over the mussels. Snip the rest of the fresh herbs over the mussels and serve at once with plenty of fresh crusty bread.

MOULES FARCIES
Stuffed Mussels

A GLORIOUS DISH. I like my stuffed mussels exceedingly garlicky, but the flavoured butter will still be delicious even if you go very easy on the garlic.

3 litres or 1.8 kg large fat
  mussels in their shells
1 large onion
1 carrot
100 ml dry white wine
1 bay leaf

Serves 4 to 6

a few sprigs each of parsley
  and thyme
freshly ground black pepper
fresh crusty bread, to serve

FOR THE STUFFING
2 to 4 cloves of garlic
several sprigs of parsley

several sprigs of chives
150 g butter, softened
60 g breadcrumbs made from
  day-old bread
sea salt
freshly ground black pepper

SCRUB THE MUSSELS WELL WITH A HARD brush under plenty of cold running water and pull off the black beards. Discard any cracked mussels and any that are still open at this stage. Keep the mussels in a large bowl of cold water.

Chop the onion and carrot. Pour the wine into a very large saucepan. Add the onion, carrot, bay leaf, parsley and thyme, then season with a little pepper.

Throw in the mussels and cook over a high heat for a few minutes until the shells open, shaking the pan occasionally. Remove the mussels from the pan with a draining spoon and discard any that are still closed. As soon as they are cool enough to handle, remove the mussels from their shells. Reserve the mussels and the bottom shells.

Heat the oven to 230°C/Gas 8. Make the stuffing. Finely chop the garlic and snip the parsley and chives very finely. Using a fork, mash together the soft butter, garlic, parsley, chives and breadcrumbs. Season with a little salt and plenty of black pepper.

Using a teaspoon or the point of a small knife, put a little flavoured butter in each half-shell. Add a mussel, then cover with a good layer of flavoured butter. Arrange the mussels in a single layer in a large gratin dish and bake for 6 to 8 minutes, until sizzling brown. Serve the mussels immediately with fresh crusty bread.

Salade de Moules aux Pommes de Terre

Mussels with Potato Salad

A SUBSTANTIAL, BUT happy combination of mussels, potatoes and mayonnaise.

3 or 4 large waxy potatoes
sea salt
90 ml olive oil
1½ tablespoons white or red
    wine vinegar
2 teaspoons mustard
freshly ground black pepper
3 litres or 1.8 kg mussels in
    their shells

Serves 6

1 large onion
1 carrot
100 ml dry white wine
several sprigs of parsley
a few sprigs of thyme
100 ml mild mayonnaise (see
    page 13)
several sprigs of chives

MAKE THE POTATO SALAD. BRING THE potatoes to the boil in plenty of lightly salted water. Reduce the heat and simmer gently until the potatoes are cooked, but still firm. Drain the potatoes and leave to cool in a colander until you can handle them comfortably. Remove the skins and cut the potatoes into medium-thick slices.

Whisk together the olive oil, vinegar and mustard. Season liberally with salt and black pepper. Distribute the dressing over the potatoes and gently turn them over until evenly coated.

Prepare and cook the mussels as described for *moules farcies* (page 63). Lift the mussels out of the cooking liquid with a draining spoon. Stir 1 to 2 tablespoons of the cooking liquid into the mayonnaise, a little at a time. Remove the mussels from their shells and discard the shells; leave to cool. Once the mussels are cold, toss them in the mayonnaise and season with freshly ground black pepper.

Heap the mussels in the centre of a round dish. Surround with the potato salad. Chop the parsley and chives and sprinkle over the potato salad. Serve at room temperature.

SOUPE DE MOULES
Mussel Soup

MY MOTHER'S RECIPE for mussel soup, full of fragrance. Both mussels and soup can be cooked several hours ahead and assembled at the last minute.

3 litres or 1.8 kg mussels in their shells 1 large onion 2 carrots 600 ml dry white wine 1 bay leaf thyme and parsley, plus extra parsley to finish freshly ground black pepper 2 leeks 2 shallots	Serves 6	30 g butter a few saffron strands 750 ml water 1 clove of garlic 6 chunky slices of French bread olive oil for sprinkling 120 ml single cream 1 large egg yolk sea salt

PREPARE AND COOK THE MUSSELS AS described for *moules farcies* (page 63); strain and reserve the cooking liquid. Remove the mussels from their shells as soon as they are cool enough to handle. Discard the shells.

Finely chop the leeks and the shallots. Melt the butter in a large saucepan. Add the saffron strands and gently sweat the chopped vegetables without letting them brown. After a few minutes, pour in the remaining 500 ml white wine, the water and the reserved cooking liquid. Bring to a simmer and cook for a few minutes.

Heat the grill. In a small bowl, snip the rest of the parsley. Cut the garlic in half and rub the bread with the cut sides of garlic. Sprinkle with olive oil and toast lightly on both sides under the grill.

Add the mussels to the liquid with half the parsley and return to a simmer. Combine the cream and the egg yolk with 1 tablespoon of the hot liquid. Stir the mixture into the soup. Check the seasoning; this soup needs plenty of freshly ground black pepper. Sprinkle with the remaining parsley and serve at once with the hot garlic toast.

Coquilles Saint-Jacques à la Crème et au Safran

Scallops with Saffron Cream

This dish is more of a main course than the other scallop recipes. Serve with long-grain rice cooked in a light stock.

Serves 4

12 to 16 scallops, off their
  shells
a few sprigs of parsley
2 tablespoons brandy
1 tablespoon olive oil
30 g butter

a pinch of powdered saffron
200 ml sour cream
1 egg yolk
sea salt
cayenne pepper

Rinse the scallops under cold running water and remove any gristle and black threads. Separate the orange coral from the white flesh and cut the flesh into 2 or 3 discs, depending on the size of the scallops. Snip the parsley into a small bowl. Put the prepared scallops and corals in a soup plate, sprinkle with brandy, cover and marinate for at least 30 minutes, turning the scallops over once or twice.

Heat the oil and butter in a sauté pan. Drain the scallops and collect the brandy juices; reserve the corals. Gently cook the slices of scallop flesh with three-quarters of the parsley in the hot oil and butter for 2 minutes, just long enough for the scallops to change colour and become firmer. Turn the scallops over once or twice during cooking. Remove them from the pan with a fish slice; set aside.

Now mash half the corals in a small bowl. Stir the saffron into the hot fat, then add the mashed corals, the cream and the brandy. bring to the boil and simmer for a couple of minutes, stirring frequently, then add the rest of the corals and cook for another minute.

Beat the egg yolk with 2 tablespoons of the hot saffron cream. Stir into the pan and reduce the heat – the mixture should no longer be allowed to boil. Continue stirring for a minute or so, then add the reserved scallop slices. Heat through and season lightly with salt and cayenne. Sprinkle with the rest of the parsley and serve.

COQUILLES SAINT-JACQUES AU BEURRE BLANC
Scallops with Shallot Butter

A CLASSIC WAY of preparing scallops and one of my favourites. The only problem is that this recipe does require constant attention. You can make the *court bouillon* and reduce the shallots well in advance, but after that, allow a totally uninterrupted quarter of an hour at the stove. The sauce will keep warm for a few minutes over hot water, but the scallops will cool quickly.

Serves 4

8 to 12 scallops, off their shells
1 onion
4 shallots
250 ml dry white wine
300 ml water
1 bouquet garni
sea salt
freshly ground black pepper
4 tablespoons white wine
    vinegar
210 g butter
a few sprigs of parsley and
    chives (optional)

MAKE A LIGHT *COURT BOUILLON*. CHOP THE onion and one of the shallots and bring to the boil in a sauté pan with the white wine, water and bouquet garni. Season and simmer for 10 minutes. Strain the liquid into a bowl; discard the onion, shallot and bouquet garni. Return the liquid to the pan.

Start preparing the shallot butter sauce. Very finely chop the rest of the shallots. Cook, with the vinegar, in a small saucepan on a moderate heat until soft and syrupy – this will take a good 15 minutes. Cut the butter into small pieces.

Rinse the scallops under cold running water, remove any gristle and black threads. Separate the orange coral from the white flesh and cut the flesh into 2 or 3 discs, depending on the size of the scallops. Add the scallops, the white flesh first, the corals after 1 minute, to the simmering liquid and

cook very gently for a few minutes – again this will depend on size, but usually 2 to 3 minutes. If the scallops aren't entirely covered by the liquid, add extra water, very hot but not boiling; do not let boil and be careful not to overcook the scallops, since this will toughen the flesh and damage the corals. Reserve 3 tablespoons of the cooking liquid. Drain the scallops and keep warm.

Meanwhile, continue cooking the sauce. Whisk the butter into the shallot purée, a few pieces at a time, without ever letting the mixture come to the boil. Whisk briskly and continuously, occasionally taking the pan off the heat. Trickle the reserved cooking liquid, a little at a time, into the finished sauce, whisking well. Check the seasoning. Snip some parsley and chives into the sauce, if you like. Spoon the sauce over the scallops just before serving.

Coquilles Saint-Jacques Surprise
Scallops with a Puff Pastry Lid

I CANNOT REMEMBER exactly where I first ate this dish. All I remember is that it was a long time ago, in someone's house and with my parents . . . I like serving seafood first courses in scallop shells and the puff pastry lids are fun to break into.
The method also works well with folded fillets of sole or turbot, perhaps with the addition of a small pinch of saffron.

8 to 12 scallops and 4 large, undamaged, saucer-shaped scallop shells	Serves 4	30 g butter sea salt
1 shallot		cayenne pepper
200 g button mushrooms	4 tablespoons dry white wine	a little flour
1 tablespoon olive oil	several sprigs of chives	300 g ready-made puff pastry 1 egg yolk

RINSE THE SCALLOPS WELL UNDER COLD running water. Remove the greyish gristle around the cushion and the black threads, then separate the coral from the white flesh and cut the flesh into 2 or 3 discs, depending on the size of the scallops. Wash the scallop shells, scrubbing them if necessary; dry well.

Steam the prepared scallops for 2 to 3 minutes over boiling water. Meanwhile, finely chop the shallot. Wipe the mushrooms and slice very thinly. Heat the oil and soften the shallot and mushrooms for a couple of minutes over a low heat. Put a baking tray in the oven and heat to 220°C/Gas 7.

Divide the shallot and mushroom mixture among the prepared shells. Cover with slices of scallop and coral. Moisten with the white wine and snip in some chives. Add a small knob of butter and season lightly with salt and cayenne.

On a lightly floured board, roll out the pastry very thinly. Cut into 4 circles, slightly larger than the scallop shells. Place a pastry 'lid' over each filled scallop shell. Score the dough attractively with a sharp knife and make a hole in the centre to let the steam escape. Now seal the pastry: press the edges down all the way around with moistened fingers and then brush the edges with a little egg yolk.

Bake for 1 minute, then remove from the oven and brush all over the pastry lids lightly with egg yolk to glaze. Bake for 7 to 8 minutes more. Serve immediately.

SAUMON CUIT AU FOUR AVEC UNE PETITE SAUCE SAFRANÉE

Roast Salmon with Saffron Sauce

ALL IT TAKES FOR A NEW DISH to become part of the family repertoire is one happy feast, with empty platters and plates scraped clean at the end of it. A few summers ago we celebrated July 14th and France's soccer World Cup success with a huge oven-roasted flounder served with saffrony juices. It had a price tag to match its size. Our favourite fishmonger in the local market (the one whose stall attracts the longest line) still grins at us fondly every time he sees us approach. *Un beau fletan?* What about a nice flounder, he asks invitingly ... More often than not we leave with somewhat humbler fry in the still handsome shape of a salmon or sea trout, both particularly good cooked this way.

If you do succumb to a flounder, roast it dark skin up for 20 to 30 minutes, until barely flaky, checking after 20 minutes lest you overcook this precious beauty.

Serves 6

1 salmon, about 1.4 kg, head
  removed, drawn, boned and
  halved lengthways
3 tablespoons olive oil
leaves from several sprigs of
  rosemary and parsley,
  snipped

white parts of 3 large spring
  onions, thinly sliced
1 unwaxed lemon, half juiced,
  half thinly sliced
60 g butter, diced
a pinch of saffron strands
sea salt
freshly ground black pepper

HEAT THE OVEN TO 200°C/GAS 6. RUB the skin of the salmon with salt and pepper, then brush with a little olive oil. Brush a baking tin with olive oil, then scatter some of the herbs and half of the lemon slices in the centre of the tin. Distribute the spring onion evenly over the top. Put the salmon on top of the spring onion, flesh sides up.

Paint the flesh side of the fish with olive oil. Scatter over a few more herbs, then season with salt and pepper. Dot a quarter of the butter over the salmon, sprinkle with half the lemon juice and season again.

Roast for about 20 minutes, until the salmon is opaque and cooked through to your liking.

Meanwhile, bring about 200 ml water to the boil. Leave the fish to settle for 5 minutes, then, using a fish slice, transfer the salmon to a warm serving dish, skin side down. Put the baking tin over a moderate heat (or pour the cooking juices into a small saucepan if your tin is not flameproof). Add the lemon juice and saffron strands and stir for a minute. Stir in the boiling water and continue stirring for a few seconds. Add the rest of the butter and whisk in. Season the sauce and strain into a warmed sauceboat. Spoon a couple of tablespoons of sauce over the salmon. Decorate with the rest of the herbs and lemon slices and serve as soon as possible.

Soupe de Poissons Madame Bastier
A Provençal Fish Soup

Cherchez le poisson – it's not easy to get *rascasse, girelles and sarans* away from the Mediterranean shores. I use a mixture of red mullet, brill, smoked cod (for its strong flavour), large prawns, monkfish and crab flesh. An extra pinch of saffron will help if you feel your ingredients are too bland.

	Serves 4	
about 1.5 kg fish, cleaned, drawn and chopped and shellfish (see above)		To serve pieces of toast rubbed with garlic (see recipe for *soupe de moules* page 65)
2 large white onions	2 to 3 tablespoons olive oil	*rouille* (page 29)
3 cloves of garlic	½ teaspoon ground saffron	
1 bulb of fennel	a bunch of thyme	
1 or 2 potatoes	2 sprigs of rosemary	
2 large ripe tomatoes	sea salt	
	freshly ground black pepper	

PREPARE THE VEGETABLES. CHOP THE onions, garlic and fennel. Peel and slice the potatoes. Blanch, peel, seed and chop the tomatoes.

In a heavy-based flameproof casserole or large saucepan, heat the oil and gently sauté the onions, garlic and fennel until very lightly browned. Stir in the fish and cook for a few minutes, then add about 1.2 litres water, the potatoes, saffron, thyme, rosemary and tomatoes. Bring to the boil, then reduce the heat and simmer for 20 to 25 minutes, until the potatoes are cooked.

Now comes the slightly messy bit of the recipe. Remove the fish and vegetable pieces from the pan with a draining spoon; pick out and discard as much skin, bones and sprigs of herbs as you can and pass the rest through a *mouli* – or whizz in a food processor. Return to the heat and finish cooking for 5 to 10 minutes. Season and serve with toast rubbed with garlic and *rouille*.

Colin Poêlé Sauce Moutarde
Pan-Fried Cod with Mustard Sauce

Friday was and still is, Fish Day in France. As goodish Catholics we religiously ate fish, but my Protestant cousins on my father's side had fish too and so did all my school friends. Perhaps it was because the fishmongers' displays were always at their shimmery best on Fridays . . .

I used to beg for sole and *langoustines*. Too expensive, said my mother. Cod was much better value and it duly appeared on the table practically every Friday lunchtime. It was pan-fried, but, alas, not accompanied by mustard sauce. I only liked the 'burned bits' and considered the dish to be the height of boring family food. It took me years, and a nice down-to-earth fishmonger's in London's Brewer Street, to enjoy cod. Pity this reliable fish had by then become so expensive. The mustard sauce is a personal favourite, evolved from a recipe my mother was very fond of. I use it with all kinds of fish, poached, broiled or pan-fried, and it is pretty good with white meat, too.

4 cod steaks
1 tablespoon flour
sea salt
cayenne pepper
dried thyme
1 tablespoon olive oil
30 g butter

Serves 4

For the mustard sauce
2 shallots
1 small bunch of flat-leaf
  parsley
60 g butter
1 tablespoon flour

250 ml double cream
1 to 1½ tablespoons Dijon
  mustard
sea salt
freshly ground black pepper
1 egg yolk
½ lemon

Dry the cod with paper towels. Season the flour with a little salt, cayenne pepper and a pinch of dried thyme.

Prepare the mustard sauce. Finely chop the shallots and snip the parsley. Melt half the butter in a small, heavy-based saucepan. Sweat the shallots and parsley in the melted butter over a low heat, making sure neither butter nor shallots change colour. Stir in the rest of the butter, then sprinkle in the flour as soon as it has melted. Cook for a couple of minutes, stirring briskly, then add the cream. Continue to cook until thick and smooth, then stir in the mustard. Taste and season well with salt and freshly ground black pepper.

Meanwhile, cook the fish. Heat the oil in a frying pan large enough to take the cod steaks comfortably. Add the butter and once it has melted, add the fish. Pan-fry the cod for about 4 minutes on each side, depending on thickness, keeping the heat moderate: the fish tends to disintegrate if you cook it too fast or too long. Turn it over carefully halfway through with a fish slice.

Just before you are ready to serve, beat the egg yolk with the juice of the ½ lemon in a small bowl. Add 2 tablespoons of the sauce, beat until combined, then stir the mixture into the saucepan. If the sauce seems too thick at this stage, thin it down with a few teaspoons of boiling water, stirred in 1 teaspoon at a time. Arrange the cod steaks on a serving dish. Spoon some of the sauce over them and sprinkle with snipped parsley. Serve the rest of the sauce separately.

Colin Poêlé Petite Sauce Moutarde
Cod Steaks with Quick-Mustard Sauce

A QUICKIE VERSION of the previous recipe. More basic, certainly, but lighter and a good simple dish.

Serves 4

4 cod steaks
1 tablespoon flour
sea salt
cayenne pepper
dried thyme
1 tablespoon olive oil
30 g butter

FOR THE QUICK-MUSTARD SAUCE
90 ml dry white wine
90 ml double cream

30 g butter
2 to 3 teaspoons Dijon mustard
sea salt
freshly ground black pepper
a few sprigs of flat-leaf
  parsley

COOK THE FISH AS IN THE PREVIOUS recipe. Remove from the frying pan with a fish slice and keep warm in the serving dish. Turn up the heat a little. Swirl the wine into the pan, then whisk in the cream and stir as the liquid reduces a little.

Cut the butter into small pieces. Stir the mustard into the sauce. Dot the butter pieces around the pan and stir until melted. Season with salt and freshly ground black pepper. Pour or spoon the sauce over the fish and snip the parsley over it. Serve immediately.

Raie au Beurre Noir
Skate in Black Butter

As I AM ONLY TOO AWARE, there is one slight problem with this justly famous dish: only a few seconds separate *beurre noir*, which is a tempting hazelnut colour, from acrid *beurre brûlé*. The only thing you can do is tip out the evil stuff, pat the pan clean with a wad of paper towels and start again.

Serves 4

1 kg skate wings
90 ml red wine vinegar
a few sprigs of thyme
1 bay leaf
1 small onion, quartered
1 small carrot, quartered

sea salt
freshly ground black pepper
several sprigs of parsley
120 g butter
3 tablespoons capers

POACH THE FISH. PLACE THE SKATE WINGS in a sauté pan large enough to take the wings comfortably. Cover with cold water, then add 2 tablespoons of vinegar, the thyme, bay leaf, onion and carrot. Season lightly with salt and freshly ground black pepper and bring to the boil over a low heat, then simmer gently for 10 to 12 minutes, until the flesh is tender enough to flake with a fork.

Snip the parsley into a bowl and melt the butter over a very low heat. Remove the skate from the pan with a fish slice, drain and remove the skin if necessary. Pat the flesh dry with paper towels. Put the fish on a serving dish and sprinkle with the parsley. Reserve a little poaching liquid.

Turn up the heat under the butter just a little and swirl the butter until it turns golden brown. Trickle half of it over the skate and parsley. Return the pan to the heat, swirl in the rest of the vinegar, the capers and a couple of tablespoons of poaching liquid. Stir until heated through, pour over the fish and serve.

LOTTE À LA PROVENÇALE
Monkfish with Tomato and Herbs

THIS UNPRETENTIOUS DISH was definitely inspired by Provence, but I cannot guarantee that it is one hundred per cent authentic . . . Use plenty of fresh herbs and very ripe tomatoes.

800 g monkfish, without skin and bones	**Serves 4**	a few sprigs of rosemary sea salt
1 large white Spanish onion	2 cloves of garlic	freshly ground black pepper
90 ml olive oil	a small bunch of parsley	150 ml dry white wine
4 ripe tomatoes	a few sprigs of fresh thyme	60 g Gruyère cheese

CUT THE FISH INTO 8 TO 10 EVEN-SIZE pieces; pat dry with paper towels. Finely chop the onion. Heat the oven to 180°C/Gas 4.

Heat half the oil in a large frying pan. Briskly sauté the fish with half the chopped onion over a moderately high heat, turning the pieces over carefully. The monkfish will soon become firmer and golden white.

Coat a large baking dish with the remaining oil. Remove the monkfish and onion from the pan with a fish slice and put them in the dish. Blanch the tomatoes, then peel and slice them thinly; discard the seeds. Arrange the tomato slices over the fish.

Finely chop the garlic. In a small bowl, snip the fresh herbs, reserving a few sprigs of parsley to finish off the dish. Add the rest of the onion and the garlic to the fresh herbs and stir well. Scatter the mixture over the fish and tomatoes. Season with salt and black pepper and pour in the wine. Grate the cheese over the dish. Bake for 15 to 20 minutes until sizzling and golden brown. Snip the rest of the parsley over the dish and serve hot.

Gratin de Haddock au Riz
Gratin of Smoked Haddock

I still have my mother's index card with her blueprint of this recipe, in her precise and elegant handwriting. She wasn't at all convinced when I told her I thought *gratin de haddock au riz* was rather like an Anglo-Indian classic called kedgeree . . . The basic ingredients may be similar, but the cheesy *gratin* method and the end result are definitely very French.

Serves 4

800 g skinned smoked haddock
   fillets
1.2 litres milk
60 g butter
grated nutmeg
1 egg
225 g long-grain rice
sea salt
90 g Gruyère or strong
   Cheddar
3 tablespoons breadcrumbs
   made from day-old bread
a small bunch of parsley
freshly ground black pepper

Rinse the haddock. In a saucepan wide enough to take the haddock fillets side by side, bring the milk to a simmer with a knob of butter and a good pinch of nutmeg. Hard-boil and then shell the egg. Meanwhile, add the haddock to the milk and poach for 5 to 8 minutes, until firm and just cooked. Lift out of the pan with a draining spoon and drain; set aside on paper towels. Reserve the milk in the pan.

Cook the rice in another saucepan for 3 minutes in lightly salted boiling water. Bring the milk back to the boil. Drain the rice and pour it into the boiling milk. Reduce the heat a little and simmer for 15 minutes, or until the rice is tender.

Heat the oven to 200°C/Gas 6. Butter a baking dish. Drain, refresh and again drain the rice, then spread it over the dish bottom; pat dry with a paper towel. Grate half the cheese over the rice. Shred the haddock, removing all the bones and spread the flakes over the rice and grated cheese.

Grate the rest of the cheese over the haddock. Sprinkle with the breadcrumbs, then snip the parsley and scatter most of it over the dish, reserving a little. Dot with small pieces of butter. Season with black pepper and bake for 5 to 10 minutes, until crisp and golden. Grate the hard-boiled egg into the bowl with the reserved parsley. Mix and sprinkle over the dish before serving.

BRANDADE DE MORUE
Salt Cod Purée

Perhaps it was because the village church wasn't heated, but, as a child, I always found Good Friday a shivery experience. The happiness of Easter Sunday seemed an intolerably long way away. The warmest thing about Good Friday was *brandade de morue*, smooth, creamy, pleasingly fishy and very comforting. The recipe below is the one I prefer. When I cooked *brandade* for my father, who had a marked fondness for *crème fraîche*, I used double the amount of cream to avoid complaints – and the irritating sight of a large undistinguished tub being ostentatiously passed around the table.

450 g salt cod
1 bouquet garni
3 cloves of garlic
200 ml olive oil
100 ml milk

Serves 4 to 6

3 tablespoons double cream
freshly ground black pepper
garlic croutons, to serve, if
   liked
butter to reheat, if wished

Soak the salt cod for at least 18 hours in plenty of cold water, changing the water several times.

Break the fish into several chunks. Place in a sauté pan with the bouquet garni, cover with cold water, bring to the boil and simmer for 10 minutes. Remove from the pan and drain well. Discard the skin and as many bones as possible and shred the salt cod very finely into a large bowl. Finely chop the garlic and gently heat the olive oil and milk in separate pans.

Put the bowl of shredded salt cod over a pan of simmering water. Gradually pour in half the warm olive oil, pounding the mixture well with a large pestle or wooden spoon. Work in the garlic, then the rest of the oil and the warm milk, a little at a time – this will take about 10 minutes and you should end up with a thick, slightly sticky, white purée.

Stir in the cream and season generously with freshly ground black pepper. Serve at once, if you like with garlic croutons. Alternatively, leave to cool completely.

To reheat, generously butter a gratin dish and spoon the *brandade* into the dish. Smooth the top and dot with butter. Reheat in the oven at 190°C/Gas 5 for 15 minutes or so before serving the dish.

Morue Parmentier
Salt Cod with Potatoes

THIS DISH REQUIRES less elbow grease than *brandade de morue*. Make sure you poach the cod very gently since it tends to toughen when boiled too fast or for too long.

Serves 4 to 6

450 g salt cod
450 g waxy potatoes
sea salt
1 bouquet garni
1 large white onion
1 tablespoon olive oil
200 ml béchamel (see page 13)
butter for greasing and to finish
cayenne pepper
45 g Gruyère or strong
    Cheddar cheese, grated
several sprigs of parsley,
    chopped
freshly ground black pepper

SOAK THE SALT COD IN PLENTY OF COLD water for at least 18 hours, changing the water several times. Cook the potatoes in barely boiling, lightly salted water until just tender. Drain, refresh and peel the potatoes as soon as they are cool enough to handle; cut them into thick slices.

While the potatoes are boiling, poach the salt cod. Break it into chunks, place in a sauté pan with the bouquet garni, cover with cold water and bring to the boil, then simmer gently for 10 minutes; drain well. Discard as much skin and bones as possible, then shred the cod.

Heat the oven to 200°C/Gas 6. Finely chop the onion. Heat the oil in a small frying pan and sweat the onion over a low heat for a few minutes, stirring frequently. Remove from the pan with a draining spoon, drain on paper towels, then stir the onion into the béchamel.

Butter a gratin dish. Spread the slices of potato over the dish. Cover with the shredded salt cod and season with a little cayenne pepper. Cover with the onion-flavoured béchamel. Scatter the cheese and parsley over the béchamel. Season with freshly ground black pepper and dot with butter. Bake until golden brown. Serve hot.

Morue en Aïoli
Salt Cod with Garlic Mayonnaise

Vary the vegetables according to what is in season. Cooked beets are a popular accompaniment.

1 kg salt cod	Serves 6	several sprigs of thyme
4 eggs		2 bay leaves
8 small potatoes		1 onion
sea salt		150 ml dry white wine
4 carrots		350 ml garlic mayonnaise (see
3 bulbs of fennel		page 13)
1 small cauliflower		2 tomatoes
400 g green beans		freshly ground black pepper

Soak the salt cod in plenty of cold water for at least 18 hours, changing the water several times.

Once the fish is de-salted, hard-boil the eggs and start preparing the vegetables. Scrub the potatoes, then cook them in lightly salted water. Peel the carrots, cut them into chunks and cook in lightly salted boiling water. Trim and halve the fennel bulbs and cook with the carrots. Cut the cauliflower into florets and cook in lightly salted water. Top and tail the beans and cook with the cauliflower florets. The vegetables should all be cooked through but not soft. Refresh them quickly under cold running water and drain well.

Now poach the fish. Break the cod into chunks. Place in a large sauté pan with the thyme, bay leaves, onion and wine. Cover with cold water, bring to the boil, turn the heat down and simmer very gently for 12 to 15 minutes, until the fish is just tender. Remove the fish from the pan, drain well, refresh and drain again; discard the skin and bones and coarsely shred the fish. Beat 1 to 2 tablespoons of the poaching liquid into the garlic mayonnaise.

Arrange the shredded salt cold in the centre of a large serving dish. Shell the hard-boiled eggs and cut them in half lengthways. Quarter and seed the tomatoes. Arrange the tomatoes and eggs around the salt cod. Surround with the cooked vegetables.

To finish, season the dish with a little freshly ground black pepper and serve with a bowl of garlic mayonnaise.

Filets de Merlan aux Petits Légumes

Baked Whiting Fillets with Vegetables

WHITING MAY NOT be many people's favourite fish, but it responds very well to the treatment below. This is a good method for cooking all the humbler varieties of whitefish. You will also find whiting labelled as silver hake.

Serves 4

200 g carrots
120 g celery
200 g brown cap mushrooms
2 shallots
45 g butter
sea salt
freshly ground black pepper
150 ml single cream
6 whiting fillets, skinned
120 ml dry white wine
a few sprigs of chervil
a few sprigs of chives

PREPARE THE VEGETABLES. PEEL THE carrots and slice into small matchsticks. Trim the celery and cut into narrow slices. Halve and finely slice the mushrooms. Finely chop the shallots.

In a sauté pan, melt half the butter and gently cook the carrots, celery and mushrooms over a low heat for about 10 minutes, stirring occasionally. Season with salt and black pepper and stir in half the cream. Cook, partly covered, for 5 minutes more, still over a low heat; do not let boil.

Heat the oven to 180°C/Gas 4. Spread the vegetables out in a baking dish large enough to hold the whiting in a single layer. Put the fillets on top of the vegetables. Sprinkle with the chopped shallots and trickle the white wine and the rest of the cream over the fish. Season lightly with salt and more generously with black pepper. Dot with the remaining butter and bake for 15 to 20 minutes, or until just cooked.

Snip the fresh herbs over the fish and serve hot.

TRUITE AUX PIGNONS
Trout with Pine Nuts

AN EASY VARIATION, which I particularly like, on the well-known theme of trout with almonds.

1 lemon	Serves 4	freshly ground black pepper
4 trout, cleaned and drawn		60 g pine nuts
a few sprigs of thyme	2 tablespoons olive oil	45 g butter
a few sprigs of marjoram	sea salt	3 tablespoons dry white wine

HEAT THE OVEN TO 190°C/GAS 5. Cut the lemon in half, then cut one half into 4 slices and squeeze the other half. Cut 4 pieces of foil large enough to envelop the trout. Place a trout in the centre of each piece of foil. Put a little thyme and marjoram inside each trout, then sprinkle the cavity with a few drops of olive oil and season with salt and freshly ground black pepper. Place a slice of lemon on each trout, sprinkle with a few pine nuts and a little olive oil and lemon juice. Season lightly.

Wrap the foil around the fish and seal well. Bake for 15 to 20 minutes, until the flesh is just tender enough to flake.

Meanwhile, melt a knob of butter in a small frying pan and sauté the rest of the pine nuts until golden. Remove from the pan with a draining spoon and drain on paper towels. Swirl the white wine into the pan, add the rest of the butter and stir until melted. Open the foil packages a little, sprinkle in the fried pine nuts, trickle in a little wine and butter sauce and serve.

TRUITE AUX CHAMPIGNONS
Trout with Mushrooms

A RECIPE BORROWED from another happy French exile in London, Marie-France Sandon. I have often prepared trout in this pleasingly different way since first tasting it at Marie-France's.

120 g button mushrooms	Serves 4	sea salt
4 shallots		freshly ground black pepper
several sprigs of fresh thyme	2 bay leaves	4 trout, cleaned and drawn
several sprigs of parsley	200 ml beer or light ale	150 ml single cream

WIPE AND THINLY SLICE THE MUSHROOMS, then chop the shallots very finely. In a sauté pan large enough to take the trout in a single layer, spread out the mushrooms and shallots. Add the thyme, parsley and bay leaves, reserving some parsley. Moisten with the beer and season with salt and freshly ground black pepper. Bring to the boil, lower the heat and simmer for about 10 minutes.

Add the fish to the pan, with just enough water to cover. Return to a simmer and poach for 10 minutes over a gentle heat, until the fish is tender enough to flake with a fork. Remove from the pan with a fish slice; drain and put on a serving dish.

Turn up the heat and boil the poaching liquid until it is reduced to about half the original quantity; discard the sprigs of herbs and the bay leaves. Stir in the cream until heated through. Pour the sauce over the fish. Snip the rest of the parsley over the dish, season again and serve immediately.

Daurade Farcie aux Amandes
Sea Bream with Almond Stuffing

W<small>HAT A CONSUMER-FRIENDLY</small> fish the sea bream is, with its firm flesh and untreacherous bones. This is a fun dish to make. The stuffing can be prepared ahead and chilled, leaving only the little surgical job and the finishing touches to do before baking. The cooked fish will stay hot enough for a good 20 minutes in the oven if need be, but cut back on the cooking time a little.

2 eggs	Serves 4 to 6	sea salt
4 tablespoons milk		freshly ground black pepper
1 thick slice of bread without		3 tablespoons breadcrumbs
the crust		made from day-old bread
1 large white Spanish onion	about 24 fresh shelled almonds	1 sea bream weighing about
1 shallot	several sprigs of parsley	800 g
1 clove of garlic	a few sprigs of thyme	45 g butter
3 tablespoons olive oil, plus	a sprig of rosemary	150 ml dry white wine, plus
extra if necessary	1 bay leaf	extra if necessary

P<small>REPARE THE STUFFING. HARD-BOIL AND</small> shell 1 egg. Heat the milk to boiling point in a small saucepan and soak the bread until cool enough to handle. Drain and squeeze with your hands to get rid of the excess moisture. Combine the onion with the shallot and garlic in a food processor. Heat 1 tablespoon of olive oil and sauté the mixture for a few minutes over a low heat, stirring frequently.

Without rinsing the bowl of the food processor, whizz half the almonds until finely ground. Add the parsley, thyme, rosemary, bay leaf, hard-boiled egg and bread and whizz, then moisten with the remaining egg. Add the sautéed onion, season lightly with salt and black pepper and whizz again.

Heat the oven to 190°C/Gas 5. Slit open the belly of the fish with a sharp knife. Wipe the cavity with paper towels, then spoon in the stuffing: the stuffing will expand during cooking, so don't pack the cavity too tightly. Sew up the slit to secure the stuffing. Coat a large baking dish with 1 tablespoon of olive oil. Put the fish in the dish and spoon any remaining stuffing around it. Brush the fish with the rest of the oil and sprinkle with the breadcrumbs. Cut the rest of the almonds into slivers and scatter over the fish. Cut the butter into small pieces and dot all over. Moisten with the white wine.

Cover the dish with foil and bake for 40 to 50 minutes, basting a few times with the cooking juices: if the dish looks too dry, add extra wine and a little more olive oil. After about 30 minutes, remove the foil to let the topping turn golden brown. Remove the thread that held the stuffing in place and serve piping hot.

Terrine de Poissons Anne-Sophie
Sole and Salmon Terrine

Cold fish terrines make good first courses for large family reunions, when you want to serve something reasonably impressive but have precious little time at the last minute. My sister's handsome dish is a reliable favourite. You can process the herbs for the sauce a little ahead, but don't whisk up the sauce until you are nearly ready to sit people down at the table.

Serves 8 to 10

45 g butter
3 small sole, skinned and
    filleted
750 g salmon steaks, skinned
    and boned
oil for greasing
12 large prawns in their shells,
    to finish the dish
a few sprigs of parsley or
    watercress, to finish the dish

For the stuffing
250 ml milk
2 tablespoons fresh white
    breadcrumbs
450 g whiting or cod, skinned
    and boned
150 g butter
2 eggs
12 egg yolks
550 ml double cream or *crème
    fraîche*
2 tablespoons brandy
sea salt

freshly ground black pepper
grated nutmeg
ground cayenne pepper

For the sauce
a large bunch of watercress
several sprigs each of parsley,
    chives and chervil
300 ml *crème fraîche*
½ lemon
freshly ground black pepper

Melt the butter in a large frying pan and gently sauté the sole fillets and salmon steaks, a few at a time, over a low heat. Leave to cool completely. Meanwhile, prepare the stuffing. Bring the milk to the boil in a small saucepan, then stir in the breadcrumbs. Reduce the heat and let the mixture thicken a little, stirring occasionally.

Chop the whiting finely in a food processor, then add the butter, eggs and egg yolks and the milk mixture and process until smooth. Tip or spoon the mixture into a large bowl and whisk in the cream, a little at a time. Trickle in the brandy, still stirring. Season lightly with salt and more generously with freshly ground black pepper. Stir in a good pinch of nutmeg and a small pinch of cayenne pepper

Heat the oven to 200°C/Gas 6. Grease a 2.5-litre loaf tin. Line the bottom with sole fillets, spread in a layer of stuffing, then a layer of salmon. Continue alternating layers, ending with a layer of stuffing. Knock the tin a couple of times on the work surface to ensure it is well packed.

Line a large baking tin with a folded newspaper. Put the loaf tin in the centre of the baking tin. Pour in the boiling water until it comes halfway up the sides of the loaf tin and cook the terrine in this *bain-marie* for approximately 1 hour, until the top of the terrine feels firm. Leave the terrine to get cool, then cover and weigh it down. Refrigerate for at least 3 hours, or up to 48 hours if you wish.

Prepare the sauce. Wash and trim the watercress and herbs; drain well and process quickly. Just before serving, whisk the *crème fraîche* in a bowl, then gradually stir in the herb mixture, whisking it well in. Squeeze in the lemon juice. Season the sauce with a little black pepper and spoon it into a sauceboat. Now unmould the terrine into the centre of a large serving dish. Surround with the prawns and sprigs of parsley or watercress. Serve with the sauce.

PAINS DE POISSON
Fish Loaves

In President de Gaulle's brave new France circa 1960, modern women like my mother, ex-career girls now full-time wives and mothers, were busy swopping colourful recipes that were at the time a little daring – in their relaxed use of canned food, spices and foreign, exotic ingredients. *Plats uniques* became the 'in thing' for dinner parties, with *paella* playing a starring role.

The following fish loaves are typical of the period. There was a sharp difference between family food – thrifty, filling but experimental – and dishes for entertaining – elaborately garnished and evidently more expensive. The basic fish loaf recipe was purely for family use. Note that it lists ketchup among its ingredients, the first recorded use of the stuff in my home-grown cards. Fish loaf and assorted jokes about yet another biblical miracle on the shores of the Loire became a family institution.

The second recipe was *pour les invités* – for guests. I still prefer it to the basic dish, but, then, wouldn't I just?

PAIN DE POISSON DE TOUS LES JOURS
Family Fish Loaf

Serves 6

450 g whitefish, skinned and
  boned
1 bay leaf
1 bouquet garni
sea salt
freshly ground black pepper
60 g tomato purée
2 tablespoons tomato ketchup
5 eggs
paprika
cayenne pepper
oil for greasing
60 g butter

Put the fish with the bay leaf and bouquet garni in a sauté pan. Cover with cold water, season with salt and freshly ground black pepper and bring to the boil, then simmer until the flesh is tender enough to flake easily. Drain well, remove any bones and put through a *mouli* or food processor. Stir in the tomato purée and ketchup.

Beat the eggs as for an omelette. Stir them into the fish mixture until well blended. Season with a good pinch of paprika and cayenne.

Heat the oven to 180°C/Gas 4. Grease a large loaf tin, about 2.5 litres. Pour the mixture into the tin. Line a large baking tin with a folded newspaper. Put the loaf tin in the centre of the baking tin. Pour boiling water to come halfway up the sides of the loaf tin and cook the fish loaf in this *bain-marie* for 40 minutes, or until firm.

Unmould the fish loaf on to a dish. Melt the butter in a small saucepan and pour over the fish loaf just before serving. Delicious with *anchoïade* (see page 35).

Posh Fish Loaf

	Serves 8	
2 large white Spanish onions		sea salt
3 tablespoons olive oil, plus		freshly ground black pepper
extra for greasing		paprika
1 kg tomatoes		cayenne pepper
1 clove of garlic		2 red peppers
several sprigs of thyme,		
marjoram and parsley	3 thin slices of cooked ham	To serve
dried oregano	200 g green olives, stoned	120 g butter
1.8 kg cod or hake, skinned	5 or 6 eggs	½ lemon or 350 ml hollandaise
and boned		(see page 12)

Prepare a tomato sauce. Chop the onions. Heat 1 tablespoon olive oil in a frying pan and sauté the onions over a low heat, stirring frequently. Blanch, skin, halve and seed the tomatoes, then chop roughly with the garlic and add to the onions. Add the herbs and cook gently for 20 to 30 minutes. Remove the sprigs of herbs from the pan, then process the sauce in a food processor or put through a *mouli.*

Meanwhile, cook the fish. Heat 1 tablespoon olive oil in a sauté pan. Cut the fish into large pieces and add these to the pan. Sauté over a gentle heat until cooked. Drain the pieces on paper towels, removing any visible bones, then put in a large bowl and shred finely with a fork. Stir the tomato sauce into the shredded fish and beat until well mixed.

Finely chop the ham and green olives, then add them to the fish and tomato mixture, stirring until combined. Beat the eggs as for an omelette. Season lightly with salt and freshly ground black pepper, then beat into the fish mixture. Season to taste with paprika and cayenne and also with salt and black pepper.

Grease a large loaf tin with the rest of the oil. Pour the mixture into the tin and bake as in the previous recipe for 30 to 40 minutes, until cooked: the fish loaf will stay warm for up to 15 minutes in the tin outside the oven.

Meanwhile, prepare the peppers. Cut them in half lengthways, remove the seeds and white cores, then char them under a hot grill until the skins blister. Leave the peppers until they are cool enough to handle, then peel off the skins. Now slice them into even-size narrow strips.

Just before serving, unmould the loaf on to a dish. Arrange the strips of red pepper on top of the loaf and around it. Melt the butter in a small saucepan, squeeze in the lemon juice and spoon it over the fish loaf and peppers; alternatively, coat with hollandaise. This dish can also be served cold with a light *rouille,* mayonnaise or *anchoïade.*

VOLAILLES ET VIANDES
Poultry, Game and Meat

THE TIMES MAY be a-changing, but the meat course still remains the centrepiece of the French meal – the dish you just don't do without, even when time and appetite are limited.

The following selection is a very personal one. I give you recipes that have been with me for much of my life and that I am always happy to cook. Pot roasts and stews tend to steal the show, perhaps because, when I close my eyes and think of a kitchen, sooner or later a large black cast-iron *cocotte* materialises. It never goes away. The *cocotte* is the crucible of the French kitchen, well-tempered and endlessly accommodating. I could go on happily about the miracles it performs, but a great deal has already been written and very well too, on the romance of the *cocotte*, so I won't dwell on it. Do go and buy one, though, or get to know yours, if you have one already. You will not regret it.

Meat is an expensive commodity, even more so if it turns out a culinary disappointment. For this reason I only buy packed supermarket meat and poultry if I have to. There is no pleasure in it. I feel very strongly that the buying of meat should be a personal transaction. As a child or teenager, when I was dispatched on a shopping expedition, I was generally trusted to return with more or less the right groceries, vegetables and fruit. Cheeses I was instructed to buy from one known shop, with the help of one particular assistant. But when it came to meat, my role was that of humble courier. The deal had always been discussed on the phone first, by my grandmother or my mother. The day's requirements had been carefully explained and the previous purchase commented on.

Whenever I go to a butcher's in France, I always feel that the standing in line is endless. The butchers and their customers seem to chat forever. It takes a while to readjust to the fact that nobody wants to rush the occasion. Buying meat is an important purchase that takes up a lot of the family's food budget. It needs to be given due consideration. Fortunately, things being what they are, standing in line at the butcher's is also a nice social occasion, time for a little moan and a good gossip . . .

CHAUDFROID DE POULET
Chicken Chaudfroid

A GOOD PARTY dish, particularly popular, if my memory serves me right, with elderly members of the family. It is a great showcase for one of my favourite herbs, tarragon, sadly neglected outside France.

	Serves 8 to 10	
2 large chickens		sea salt
2 carrots		freshly ground black pepper
2 turnips		60 g butter
2 leeks		60 g flour
1 onion		300 ml *crème fraîche* or double
several sprigs of parsley and		cream
tarragon, plus extra tarragon	3 cloves	4 egg yolks
to finish the dish	250 ml white wine	1 or 2 lemons

THE DAY BEFORE YOU INTEND TO SERVE the dish, place the chickens side by side in a very large, heavy-based saucepan. Peel, wash and coarsely chop the carrots, turnips, leeks and onion. Add to the pan with the parsley, tarragon and cloves. Pour in the wine and enough cold water to cover the chickens and vegetables.

Bring gently to the boil, skimming off any scum that comes up to the surface; season lightly with salt and freshly ground black pepper. Simmer for 45 to 60 minutes over a very moderate heat, until the chickens are cooked through. Leave them in the liquid until cool enough to handle, then lift the chickens out of the pot, drain well and remove the skins. Leave the birds to get cold before jointing them as neatly as possible.

Meanwhile, vigorously boil the stock for 45 to 60 minutes until reduced by a third. Leave to cool. Carefully strain the stock into a saucepan through a strainer lined with muslin or fine cloth; reserve.

To make the sauce, bring the reserved stock to a simmer; take off the heat. Melt the butter in another saucepan. Add the flour and cook for a couple of minutes, stirring vigorously to make a light roux. Pour in the hot chicken stock gradually, then bring to the boil, still stirring vigorously. Reduce the heat and simmer for about 10 minutes, stirring occasionally.

Remove the pan from the heat and leave to cool a little. Stir the cream into the sauce. Beat the egg yolks and squeeze the lemon or lemons. Beat a couple of spoonfuls of the hot sauce into the egg yolks, then stir the mixture into the sauce and continue stirring for a while. Season to taste with lemon juice, salt and freshly ground black pepper.

Pat the chicken pieces dry with paper towels and arrange them on a large serving dish. Using a ladle, coat the chicken evenly with the sauce. Chill the dish overnight and just before serving, sprinkle with the remaining tarragon leaves.

La Poule au Pot Farcie
Stuffed Boiled Chicken

A GREAT ONE-POT DISH. All it takes is a little patience as the chicken must be allowed to simmer extremely slowly indeed. If giblets aren't available, use 1 slice each of cured ham and smoked bacon, or garlic mayonnaise, or *pistou* sauce.

Serves 6

1 large chicken, with its giblets
  for the stuffing (if available)
¼ Savoy or white cabbage
sea salt
450 g carrots
400 g turnips
10 small to medium leeks
1 head of celery
several sprigs of parsley and
  thyme
2 bay leaves
freshly ground black pepper

FOR THE STUFFING
225 g thick-cut smoked bacon
200 g cooked ham

200 g breadcrumbs made from
  day-old bread
2 cloves of garlic
several sprigs of parsley
2 eggs
sea salt
freshly ground black pepper

TO SERVE
gherkins
mustard
coarse kosher salt

PREPARE THE STUFFING. COMBINE THE liver, heart and gizzard with the bacon, ham, breadcrumbs, garlic and parsley in a food processor. Add the eggs to the bowl and process briefly. Season lightly with salt and more generously with freshly ground black pepper. Spoon the stuffing into the chicken's cavity. Sew up the cavity with a trussing needle and fine string, then truss the chicken with string.

Put the chicken in a very large, heavy-based saucepan or flameproof casserole. Cover with cold water and very gently bring to the boil over a low heat, skimming the surface as and when necessary.

Prepare the vegetables while the bird is coming to the boil. Blanch the cabbage for a few minutes in lightly salted boiling water. Peel the carrots and turnips. Carefully wash and trim the leeks and celery. Tie all the vegetables together in bundles.

After the chicken has simmered for 30 minutes, add the vegetables to the pot. Season with salt. Bring back to a low boil and simmer for 1½ hours, skimming whenever necessary.

Just before serving, remove the chicken from the pot. Discard the strings and remove the stuffing from the bird, then cut the stuffing into pieces (it may fall apart a little). Serve the chicken in a large dish surrounded by the vegetables and stuffing. Strain the cooking liquid through a strainer, lined with muslin or a fine cloth. Check the seasoning and use a little strained liquid to moisten the bird and vegetables. Transfer the rest to a sauceboat. Serve with gherkins, mustard and coarse sea salt.

POULET AU VINAIGRE
Chicken with a Vinegar Sauce

ALONG WITH *FLIC*, *POULET* is one of the many words the French use to refer to a member of their police force. Moviemaker Claude Chabrol called one of his enjoyable piquant thrillers *Poulet au Vinaigre* – which somebody cleverly rendered into English as *Cop au Vin*, very passable menu French, if you ask me. I have wondered ever since if Monsieur Chabrol, a gourmet of great repute, had any strong views on the dish. This is not his recipe.

Serves 4 to 6

1 large chicken
2 tablespoons olive oil
15 g butter
2 cloves of garlic
sea salt
freshly ground black pepper
1 tablespoon Dijon mustard
1 tablespoon tomato purée
3 tablespoons dry white wine
4 tablespoons good quality
   white wine vinegar
3 tablespoons double cream

JOINT THE CHICKEN. HEAT THE OIL AND butter in a large sauté pan. Cut the cloves of garlic in half. Put the jointed chicken in the pan with the garlic and sauté for several minutes, turning the pieces over to colour lightly and evenly. Season sparsely with salt and freshly ground black pepper, cover and cook gently for 20 to 30 minutes, until the chicken pieces are cooked through; keep the heat low and shake the pan several times during the cooking.

Meanwhile, mix together in a bowl the mustard, tomato purée and white wine. When the chicken is cooked, sprinkle the vinegar into the pan; stir for a few minutes until the liquid has reduced. Cover and leave over a low heat.

Remove the chicken from the pan and keep warm. Add the mustard mixture to the pan, turn up the heat a little and stir for a couple of minutes. Spoon in the cream and heat through gently, stirring occasionally. Pour the sauce over the chicken and serve immediately.

COQ AU VIN
Chicken Cooked in Red Wine

I LOVE COOKING casseroles on top of the stove, lifting the lid, nosing the mixture and giving it an encouraging stir or two, as it melts and blends into a rich, comforting dish. *Coq au vin* is one of my favourites. I find it so enjoyable to rediscover that I never quite cook it exactly the same way. The addition of chocolate to the ingredients is a recent one, inspired by South American cooking and – closer to home – reading Raymonde Charlon, formerly of *La Godille* in Brittany. Madame Charlon's little trick does add a distinct *je ne sais quoi* to the old classic.

Serves 6

1 large chicken
2 tablespoons oil
30 g butter, plus extra to finish
   the sauce
120 g thick-cut smoked bacon
1 large white Spanish onion
2 shallots

90 ml brandy
1 tablespoon flour
600 ml Burgundy red wine
2 cloves of garlic

225 g button mushrooms
30 g dark plain chocolate
a few sprigs each of parsley
   and thyme
2 bay leaves
sea salt
freshly ground black pepper

JOINT THE CHICKEN. HEAT THE OIL AND butter in a large flameproof casserole or heavy-based saucepan. Chop the bacon, onion and shallots and sauté in the hot oil until lightly coloured. Push to the side and add the chicken pieces. Sauté the chicken until golden, turning the pieces over to colour evenly.

As soon as the chicken is a nice golden colour, pour in the brandy and set alight. Once the flames have died down, sprinkle in flour and stir well with a wooden spoon. Pour in the wine. Finely chop the garlic, slice the mushrooms and roughly grate the chocolate. Add them to the chicken with the sprigs of herbs and the bay leaves; stir well.

Turn up the heat and bring to a fast simmer, then cover and reduce the heat to moderately low. Cook for a good 30 minutes or until the chicken pieces are cooked, shaking the pan occasionally. Season to taste with salt and freshly ground black pepper. This dish tastes even better reheated and will benefit from being made in the morning – or even one day ahead. Reheat very gently, adding a little water if necessary – but not too much.

Remove the chicken pieces with tongs and put them on a plate; keep warm and discard the sprigs of herbs and bay leaves.

Turn up the heat and reduce the sauce if it looks too thin, scraping the bottom of the casserole with a wooden spoon or spatula. Stir in a good knob of butter, then return the chicken to the casserole and serve at once.

Poularde à la Tourangelle
Chicken Cooked in a Wine and Cream Sauce

A DELICATE *FRICASSÉE* FROM THE LOIRE, where it is often made with guinea fowl and Vouvray rather than just chicken and white wine. For me, this dish typifies the cooking of the area – fragrant, unpretentious and making the most of the excellent local produce.

1 chicken or guinea fowl,
    without giblets
1 tablespooon oil
45 g butter
1 onion
2 slices of thick-cut bacon
1 clove of garlic

Serves 4

150 g button mushrooms
several sprigs each of thyme,
    parsley and chives

sea salt
freshly ground black pepper
120 ml Vouvray or medium-
    dry white wine
90 ml single cream
1 lemon
2 small egg yolks

JOINT THE BIRD AND SOAK THE PIECES FOR a couple of hours in water at room temperature. Drain well and pat dry firmly with a clean cloth or paper towels.

In a sauté pan, heat the oil and butter. Chop the onion and bacon. Sauté in the pan for a few minutes over a gentle heat, then push to the sides and add the chicken pieces. Sauté until they are lightly coloured all over.

Meanwhile, crush the garlic and slice the mushrooms. Add to the pan with the fresh herbs. Season lightly with salt and freshly ground black pepper. Moisten with the white wine, then partly cover the pan and cook over a low heat until the chicken is cooked and the liquid well reduced; this takes about 20 to 30 minutes.

Pour the cream into the pan and stir until it is heated through, then remove the chicken from the pan with tongs or a draining spoon; keep warm on a serving dish. Squeeze the lemon and mix the juice with the egg yolks. Away from the heat, stir this mixture into the pan. Check the seasoning and spoon the sauce over the chicken. Serve immediately.

POULET CHASSEUR
Huntsman's Chicken

WHEN I FIRST ate *poulet chasseur*, I was also at the time endlessly listening to the first record I ever owned, *Peter and the Wolf*, narrated by Gérard Philipe (taking time off from *Fanfan La Tulipe*). So the dish stayed linked in my mind with the sound of horns and the picture of three very Russian huntsmen stalking through a forest. By the time I came across *pollo cacciatore* years later and opened my pocket Italian dictionary, I was ready to enjoy the fact that huntsmen and country dishes, like fairy tales, have much in common the world over.

4 chicken leg portions
1 tablespoon oil
30 g butter, plus extra to finish
3 shallots
1 clove of garlic
1 level tablespoon flour

Serves 4

3 tablespoons brandy
90 ml dry white wine
chicken stock or water

sea salt
freshly ground black pepper
2 tomatoes
120 g brown cap mushrooms
several sprigs of chervil and
   tarragon

HEAT THE OIL AND BUTTER. FINELY CHOP the shallots and garlic. Sauté the chicken pieces in the hot fat with the chopped shallots and garlic, turning the pieces over so that they colour evenly.

Sprinkle the chicken pieces with the flour. Add the brandy, then the white wine and enough chicken stock or water to just cover the chicken; stir well. Season with salt and freshly ground black pepper, cover and simmer over a moderate heat for 20 to 30 minutes. Shake the pan occasionally as the chicken is cooking.

Meanwhile, blanch, skin, seed and chop the tomatoes and slice the mushrooms. Stir the tomatoes and mushrooms into the pan. Cover and simmer for 10 minutes, or until the chicken is cooked through. Remove the chicken from the pan and arrange on a serving dish; keep warm while you finish off the sauce. Turn up the heat to reduce the sauce. Snip the chervil and tarragon into the pan and stir well for a minute or two, then swirl in a good knob of butter. Check the seasoning and pour the sauce over the chicken pieces. Serve immediately.

Petit Confit de Canard
Quick Duck Confit

The French 'colony' in London is large and thriving. For a few years now I have been hosting cookery sessions for an enthusiastic group of expatriate French women known as Le Cooking Club de Londres Accueil. The idea is that I demonstrate four or five dishes and then produce lunch with the help of my friend Marie-Laure. I end up hoarse-voiced after talking over the noise generated by an audience of a dozen *bavardes* torn between discussing new recipe ideas and catching up on gossip. My guinea pigs are frank and vocal about which of my dishes pass the test. They also generously contribute to my stock of recipes. This one is Brigitte Castaing's deliciously easy and light take on duck confit. I have also cooked it successfully with rabbit and free-range chicken (use large birds and reduce the cooking time by 30 minutes if cooking drumsticks rather than leg portions).

Serves 4 to 6

3 heaped tablespoons coarse kosher salt several sprigs thyme, chopped	2 teaspoons Chinese five-spice powder 6 duck leg portions	about 1 litre sunflower oil or mild-flavoured olive oil freshly ground black pepper

In a bowl, mix the salt, chopped thyme and five-spice powder. Using a sharp knife, make a few small slits through the duck skin into the flesh. Rub the duck with the seasoned salt, pressing well. Cover and chill for at least 2 hours, or up to 24 hours if convenient.

Rinse the duck under cold running water. Drain and pat dry with a clean towel. Cut off any loose bits of skin.

Heat the oven to 140°C/Gas 1. Put the duck in a deep ovenproof pot just large enough to take the pieces side by side. Pour in the oil – you should have about 5 cm of oil on top of the duck. The exact amount of oil you need depends on the pot you use – make sure there is a clear 5 cm between the surface of the oil and the rim of the pot. Put in the oven and cook uncovered for 2½ hours, turning the pieces over once after about 1½ hours.

Lift the pieces from the oil and drain well, then place on a clean towel or a thick layer of paper towels. Pat to get rid of excess oil. Season generously with black pepper. Serve as soon as possible with *gratin dauphinois* (see page 122) or *pommes de terre sautées Tata Baucher* (see page 124).

The confit freezes well and can be reheated with 1 tablespoon of the oil used for cooking in a large frying pan. Once drained through a strainer, the rest of the oil can be used again for frying potatoes and cooking another confit.

Perdreaux en Casserole
Pot-Roasted Partridges

A RECIPE FROM MY MOTHER. The sauce is best finished off with slightly bitter orange juice. So, if Sevilles aren't in season, taste it and, if it seems on the sweet side, add a dash of lemon or grapefruit juice.

60 g butter
2 oven-ready partridges
a few sprigs of parsley and
   thyme
1 bay leaf
1 heaped tablespoon flour
250 ml white wine

Serves 4

sea salt
freshly ground black pepper
cayenne pepper
120 g cured ham, thinly cut
2 Seville oranges, or 1 large
   juicy orange

ORANGES DE BLANCHARD

HEAT THE BUTTER IN A FLAMEPROOF casserole. Over a moderate heat, sauté the partridges until brown on all sides. Remove them from the pan with a draining spoon, allowing the juices to drip back into the pan. Reserve the partridges. Carefully snip the parsley, thyme and bay leaf.

Sprinkle the flour into the pan and stir until slightly coloured, then pour in the white wine and add the herbs. Season with very little salt and freshly ground black pepper and a small pinch of cayenne. Cook, stirring vigorously, until the liquid begins to bubble. Reduce the heat a little and simmer for a good 5 minutes, stirring occasionally. Return the partridges to the pan, cover and simmer very gently over a low heat for about 20 minutes.

Meanwhile, chop the ham into small pieces. Squeeze the juice from the orange or oranges into a bowl.

Transfer the partridges on to a hot serving dish. Add the ham and orange juice to the pan, stir until heated through, scraping up the sediments from the bottom of the pan. Pour the sauce over the partridges. Serve immediately.

Magrets de Canard à l'Orange
Duck Breasts with Orange

Canard à l'orange had become such a tired cliché by the early 1980s that we all heaved a sigh of relief when it was knocked off the menu by very rare *magrets* dramatically arranged on a bed of red fruit sauce. Now that these too have palled, may I suggest these duck breasts with orange? They are quick to cook, quicker still if, unlike me, you prefer them very pink. The little orange, lemon, and Cointreau sauce is adapted from my mother's much sweeter original recipe.

Serves 4

2 large, boned duck breasts,
   each weighing about
    350 g
sea salt
freshly ground black pepper
2 oranges
1 lemon
1 scant teaspoon cornflour
30 g chilled unsalted butter,
   diced
4 tablespoons Cointreau

With a small and very sharp knife, score the skin side of the duck breasts – deeply enough to cut into the flesh – several times in long parallel lines. Season with salt and freshly ground black pepper. Heat a heavy-based frying pan until hot. Put the breasts in the pan skin side down. There is enough fat in the skin not to need any more fat. Cook for a good 10 to 15 minutes over a moderate heat.

Meanwhile, peel one of the oranges and the lemon. Chop the zests very finely and blanch for a couple of minutes in a little boiling water; drain well. Squeeze the oranges and lemon.

After about 10 minutes, discard any excess fat and turn over the duck breasts. Lower the heat and cook them for 3 to 5 minutes on the flesh side – the timing will depend on how well cooked you like your duck. Remove the breasts from the pan and set aside to relax, keeping them hot on a heated serving dish under a heated plate.

Stir in the cornflour and butter, then add the orange and lemon juices and the drained, finely chopped zest. Stir for a couple of minutes over a moderate heat, until simmering. Add the Cointreau and season with a little salt and more generously with freshly ground black pepper. Spoon or pour the sauce over the duck breasts and serve immediately.

Carnard aux Pêches
Roast Duck with Peaches

My father's recipe and very good and mellow it is, too. Peaches canned in juice are worth looking for, otherwise rinse the peaches quickly under the tap (after draining off the syrup) to get rid of the excess sweetness. If fresh peaches are available, peel (see page 138) and use them.

1.8- to 2.3-kg oven-ready duck
sea salt
freshly ground black pepper

Serves 4

1 large can white peaches,
    drained and halved
3 tablespoons double cream
3 tablespoons brandy

Heat the oven to 180°C/Gas 4. Rinse the duck well inside and out and pat dry with a paper towel. Score the skin with a sharp knife. Season well inside and out with salt and freshly ground black pepper.

Stuff the cavity through the tail end with the cream and some of the peaches, reserving the rest. Put the duck on a rack in a baking tin and roast in the oven for 1½ hours. After half an hour, prick the skin, baste the duck with the cooking juices and add the rest of the peaches to the baking tin. Baste the duck again occasionally.

When the duck is cooked through, lift the rack off the baking tin. Arrange the peaches from the baking tin on a serving dish; discard much of the fat. Spoon the stuffing out of the cavity into the baking tin. Add the duck and the peaches used in the stuffing to the serving dish. Place the tin over a moderate heat and pour in the brandy. Stir the mixture for 2 minutes, scraping the bottom of the tin. Strain the sauce into a sauceboat, season to taste and serve.

Canard aux Olives
Duck with Olives

I sometimes use the same method for chicken and serve it with rice and mushrooms.

1.8- to 2.3-kg oven-ready duck
sea salt
freshly ground black pepper
1 tablespoon oil

Serves 4

30 g butter
300 ml dry white wine
a few sprigs of thyme

1 bay leaf
1 large white Spanish onion
2 large tomatoes
225 g stoned green olives

Rinse and season the duck as above. In a large, flameproof casserole, heat the oil and butter. Sauté the duck in the hot fat until the skin is crisp and golden on all sides.

Spoon a couple of tablespoons of hot fat into a frying pan and discard the rest. Add the wine and herbs, cover and reduce the heat. Cook for 30 minutes, basting twice.

Meanwhile, chop the onion and tomatoes and sauté in the reserved duck fat over a low heat until soft, stirring occasionally. Stir the onion and tomato mixture into the pot, then cover and simmer for 30 minutes more.

Stir in the olives and a little water if the mixture looks too dry. Cover and simmer for another 30 minutes. Serve very hot.

CANARD AUX NAVETS
Braised Duck with Turnips

I DON'T KNOW where the marriage of duck and turnips was made, but it is certainly a happy one. Having tried a number of approaches to the dish, I now think that dividing the turnips between the pot and the frying pan produces the best results, even if it is slightly more fiddly. If you don't like turnips, replace them with fleshy fat mushrooms, parsnips (not at all French, but never mind), or baby onions.

1.8- to 2.3-kg oven-ready duck	Serves 4 or 5	30 g butter, plus extra to finish
sea salt		the sauce
freshly ground black pepper		250 ml chicken or vegetable
1 kg baby turnips		stock
1 tablespoon oil		2 or 3 teaspoons sugar
		4 tablespoons white wine

RINSE THE DUCK WELL INSIDE AND OUT, and pat dry with paper towels. Season well inside and out with salt and freshly ground black pepper. Peel the turnips and cut them neatly into halves or quarters, depending on size. Reserve 8 to 10 pieces and cook the rest of the turnips in lightly salted boiling water for 5 to 10 minutes.

Meanwhile, in a large, flameproof casserole or heavy-based saucepan, heat the oil and butter. Sauté the duck in the hot fat until lightly golden on all sides. Pour out the fat into a frying pan to use for browning the turnips. Add the stock and the reserved turnips to the pan with the duck. Cover and cook over a low heat for about 1½ hours.

Drain the first batch of turnips and set aside. When the duck is nearly cooked, heat the fat in the frying pan and add the turnips. Sprinkle them with the sugar and sauté gently for 15 to 20 minutes over a low heat, shaking the pan occasionally and turning the turnips over.

Remove the duck from its pan and arrange it and the sautéed turnips on a serving dish; keep this dish warm. Turn up the heat, add the white wine to the duck stock and let the cooking liquid reduce a little, stirring well and mashing the turnips roughly with the back of a wooden spoon. Season with salt and freshly ground black pepper. Strain some of the sauce over the duck and the rest into a bowl or sauceboat, discarding the remaining mashed turnips. Stir a little butter into the sauceboat to finish and serve hot with the duck and turnips.

Faisan Rôti Farci
Stuffed Roast Pheasant

Like millions of other Frenchmen, my father used to go shooting regularly on a Sunday, so pheasant often featured on our menu during the autumn and winter months. Far too often it seemed, to his daughters, because we much preferred chicken and said so loudly every time its elegant relative appeared on the table. In the end my mother gave up setting pearls in front of her piglets and served pheasant to her dinner party guests instead.

1 plump pheasant, dressed,
  gizzards reserved
4 thin slices unsmoked bacon
1 extremely small jar or can of
  truffle parings
3 tablespoons brandy

Serves 2 to 4

1 tablespoon breadcrumbs
  made from day-old bread
75 g butter
sea salt
freshly ground black pepper
4 thick pieces of bread

Heat the oven to 220°C/Gas 7 and then prepare the stuffing. Rinse the gizzards and process them quickly with 1 slice of bacon, the truffle parings and their juice, 1 tablespoon of brandy, the breadcrumbs and a good knob of butter in a food processor. Season with a little salt and freshly ground black pepper. Rinse the cavity of the pheasant and pat it dry with paper towels. Spoon the stuffing into the cavity, then sew it up, using a trussing needle and fine string.

Stretch the remaining bacon slices with the help of a rolling pin or metal spatula. Wrap the bird well in the bacon and tie with string.

Toast the bread very lightly. Melt the rest of the butter in a small saucepan. Lay the toasted bread pieces on the bottom of a roasting tin. Stand a rack in the tin and place the pheasant on the rack. Trickle a little melted butter over the pheasant. Keep the melted butter warm.

Roast the pheasant in the oven for about 50 minutes, occasionally dribbling more melted butter over it. If the bread looks as if it is about to burn, remove it from the tin and reserve in a warm place. Remove the bacon larding and discard with the strings, or reserve the bacon for a salad. Add the rest of the brandy to the melted butter. Return the bread to the tin, if necessary. Dribble the butter and brandy over the pheasant, season lightly with salt and freshly ground black pepper and return to the oven for 5 to 10 minutes more, until golden brown.

To serve, cut off and discard the string. Extract the stuffing and divide it between the pieces of buttery toast. Arrange the toast, stuffing and pheasant on a dish. Serve hot.

Terrine de Faisan
Pheasant Terrine

La terrine maison. We tended to help ourselves from the dish, not terribly elegantly and served bread, butter and gherkins with this. For special occasions, however, this terrine looks most presentable, unmoulded on to a gleaming platter, cut into thin overlapping slices and surrounded by a small border of chopped aspic and a tiny bouquet of parsley.

Serves 8

1 plump pheasant
500 g spare rib of pork
a few sprigs of thyme
3 sage leaves
1 bay leaf
3 cloves of garlic
sea salt
freshly ground black pepper

90 ml brandy or marc
2 medium eggs
6 thin slices of smoked bacon

FOR THE ASPIC
2 carrots
several sprigs of thyme, parsley
  and chervil

1 bay leaf
6 black peppercorns
300 ml dry white wine
30 g good unflavoured aspic
  powder
2 teaspoons brandy
2 tablespoons Madeira wine

HEAT THE OVEN TO 170°C/GAS 3. JOINT and bone the pheasant. Reserve the breast fillets and also set aside the bones. Bone and trim the pork, again reserving the bones.

Finely mince, or quickly whizz together in a food processor, the pheasant meat, including the liver, the pork, thyme, sage and bay leaves and the garlic. Season the meat mixture with salt and more generously with freshly ground black pepper. Stir in the brandy and the eggs and work the mixture well, preferably with your hands.

Stretch the bacon slices with the help of a rolling pin or metal spatula. Line a terrine dish (or a loaf tin) with a couple of bacon slices, then spread in an even layer of meat and egg mixture. Cut the breast fillets into neat long strips and place 2 or 3 strips over the meat and egg layer. Cover with another layer of breast fillets on top. Spread in another layer of meat mixture, then cover with bacon rashers. Cover the dish tightly.

Line a large roasting tin with a thick layer of newspapers. Place the dish in the middle of the tin. Pour in boiling water to come halfway up the sides of the dish. Carefully put the tin in the oven and bake for a good 3 hours, pouring in more boiling water as

and when necessary to keep the halfway level.

While the terrine is in the oven, prepare the aspic. Peel the carrots. Put the reserved bones in a large saucepan with the peeled carrots, the sprigs of herbs, the bay leaf and the peppercorns. Cover with the white wine and 850 ml cold water. Slowly bring to the boil, skimming off any greasy scum that comes up to the surface. Partly cover and simmer for a couple of hours, skimming off occasionally. Turn up the heat towards the end – you should end up with 600 ml stock. Strain through a strainer lined with muslin, or through a *chinois*, into a bowl. Stand in cold water to cool.

Leave the terrine to relax in the oven for 15 minutes after you turn off the heat. Remove from the oven, take off the cover and leave for a few minutes. Meanwhile, transfer the stock to a saucepan and make the aspic following the package instructions. Stir in the brandy and Madeira wine.

Remove the bacon slices from the top of the terrine. Pierce the meat deeply in several places with a skewer. Pour the warm aspic liquid over the meat. Leave to cool and refrigerate overnight.

Lapin en Daube
Pot-Roasted Rabbit

A USEFUL DISH that slowly cooks all by itself. I have been vaguer than usual about the timing, since it will depend entirely on the age and provenance of your rabbit. If you prefer, follow exactly the same method, but use hare, kid or chicken.

Serves 4

1 rabbit, jointed, or 4 to 6
  rabbit pieces
6 thick-cut slices smoked
  bacon
1 large white Spanish onion
1 carrot
several sprigs each of parsley,
  thyme and rosemary
2 bay leaves
3 juniper berries
2 cloves of garlic
sea salt
freshly ground black pepper
150 ml dry white wine

HEAT THE OVEN TO 150°C/GAS 2. Flatten and stretch the slices of bacon with the help of a rolling pin – I wrap my old wooden one in plastic wrap first in the interests of hygiene. Line the bottom of a medium-size casserole with 3 slices and reserve the rest.

Slice the onion and carrot and arrange the slices on the bacon. Snip half the herbs over the vegetables and add the rabbit pieces, then the bay leaves and juniper berries. Crush the garlic and put on top of the rabbit pieces. Snip the rest of the herbs on to the rabbit pieces. Season with a little salt and more generously with freshly ground black pepper. Moisten with the wine. Cover with the rest of the bacon slices.

Cover the dish and cook in the oven for 2 to 3 hours, until the rabbit is very tender. Serve piping hot.

Lapin à la Moutarde
Rabbit with Mustard

I still love mustard and am known to use it surreptitiously with roast chicken or lamb, but over the years, my *lapin à la moutarde* has become gradually milder. The recipe below is the state of the art at the moment. In the old days, I stirred in an extra couple of tablespoons of milder mustard before adding the liquid to the browned and floured rabbit. Try it both ways and also experiment with different mustards until you get the results you like best.

Serves 4

1 rabbit, jointed, or 4 to 6
  rabbit pieces
1 tablespoon oil
45 g butter, plus extra to finish
sea salt
freshly ground black pepper
1 tablespoon flour

1 clove of garlic
2 shallots
a few sprigs each of thyme and
  rosemary
200 ml chicken stock or white
  wine, plus extra liquid if
  needed

3 tablespoons brandy
3 tablespoons strong Dijon
  mustard, or your favourite
  mustard
120 ml single cream
a few sprigs of parsley, to finish

Heat the oil and butter in a flameproof casserole or sauté pan. Add the rabbit pieces to the pan, season with salt and freshly ground black pepper and sprinkle in the flour. Sauté for a few minutes, turning the pieces over regularly. Crush the garlic and finely chop the shallots. Add to the pan. Snip in the thyme and rosemary.

Moisten with the chicken stock or white wine, stir and cook, covered, over a low heat for about 45 minutes – the exact timing will depend on the rabbit you are using. Shake the pan occasionally and reduce the heat if necessary – rabbit pieces tend to shred and stick all too easily to the bottom of pans. Moisten with a little extra liquid if needed. Heat the brandy and pour it over the rabbit. Set alight, then remove the rabbit pieces from the pan and keep them warm on a plate or serving dish while you finish the sauce.

Remove the sprigs of thyme and rosemary. Stir in the mustard and the cream. Heat for a couple of minutes, still stirring.

Snip in the parsley and swirl in a good-size knob of butter, then pour the sauce over the rabbit. If you prefer to serve the rabbit from the pan, gently stir the pieces into the sauce instead.

Lapin à la Bière et aux Pruneaux
Rabbit with Ale and Prunes

Having once overheard grown-ups exchanging dire tales of myxomatosis and not realizing that they were reminiscing and that the big epidemic was a thing of the past, I spent my childhood carefully avoiding rabbits, both in the hutch and on the plate. What a good thing I missed out on! This recipe converted me in the end. If you share my early phobia, don't give up on this rich, dark dish. For rabbit read pork, or stewing steak. The recipe is excellent for cheaper cuts of beef; trim off as much visible fat as possible, and double the cooking time.

1 rabbit, about 800 g, cut into 4
   to 6 pieces
flour for coating
2 tablespoons oil
225 g thick-cut smoked bacon
1 onion
several sprigs of thyme

Serves 4

2 bay leaves
600 ml brown ale
175 g moist stoned prunes
2 tablespoons wine vinegar

sea salt
freshly ground black pepper

To serve
1 large slice *pain de campagne*
   or mixed-grain toast
Dijon mustard

Coat the rabbit pieces lightly with flour. Heat the oil in a heavy-based flameproof casserole or large saucepan. Add the rabbit pieces and gently sauté until golden, turning them over to brown evenly.

Cut the bacon into small 2.5-cm pieces and chop the onion. Add bacon and onion to the sautéed rabbit pieces with the thyme and bay leaves. Sprinkle with a little flour and stir well, then pour in the ale. Partly cover

the casserole and cook for about 40 minutes over a low heat. Add the prunes and wine vinegar, give a good stir and continue to cook for 20 minutes. Again, leave the lid only partly covering the pot.

Taste and season the sauce. Generously spread Dijon mustard over both sides of the piece of toast and add to the casserole. Cover completely and cook for 10 minutes more before serving.

CIVET DE LIÈVRE
Jugged Hare

To MAKE A PROPER jugged hare, you need to collect the blood as you skin and gut the animal. This you use to make a liaison, which enriches and finishes off this 'noble dish'. You also need 'your two best bottles of red wine'. The incomparable Edouard de Pomiane, whose words I am humbly borrowing, had only one regret – that he was not wealthy enough to 'make a *civet* with Chambertin' . . . . Back in Touraine, we used Bourgueil, one bottle to cook with and one (or two) to drink with the dish.

If you aren't able to get hold of a whole hare, complete with blood, use a little *beurre manié* made by mashing together flour and butter (see page 12) to thicken the sauce. And if you can't find a hare, use rabbit instead. The marinade does wonders for even the toughest of bunnies. It won't be quite the real thing, but it will still be a marvellous casserole.

This dish is traditionally served with croutons.

	Serves 6	
1 hare		1 tablespoon oil
1 bottle of good red wine		45 g butter
4 tablespoons brandy		1 tablespoon flour
2 cloves of garlic	3 bay leaves	sea salt
1 large white Spanish onion	6 black peppercorns	freshly ground black pepper
several sprigs each of thyme	4 thick-cut slices of smoked	225 g button mushrooms
and parsley	bacon	croutons, to serve, if liked

CAREFULLY SKIN AND GUT THE HARE; collect all the blood you can into a bowl. Devein the liver if necessary, also cutting out any yellowish bits and add it to the blood; cover and chill until needed. Joint the animal, cutting the back pieces with the help of your strongest knife and a mallet – or make a deal with your friendly local butcher.

Put the pieces of hare in a deep dish and cover with the wine and brandy. Finely chop the garlic and onion and snip the thyme and parsley, then add them all to the marinade, with the bay leaves and peppercorns. Marinate for 24 hours in a cool place.

A few hours before you intend to serve the hare, chop the bacon. Remove the hare from the marinade, drain well and pat dry with a clean towel or paper towels. Reserve the marinade.

Heat the oil and butter in a casserole or large sauté pan. Put the chopped bacon in the pan and stir over a medium heat for a couple of minutes, then add the hare. Stir for 5 to 10 minutes until the meat begins to turn brown. Sprinkle in the flour and stir for a minute, then pour in the marinade. Season to taste, stir, cover and cook over a low heat for at least 1 hour, perhaps 2 – the meat is cooked when it begins to come off the bones easily.

Slice the mushrooms and stir them into the pan towards the end of cooking. Remove the reserved liver from the bowl, chop it very finely and stir it into the pan. Simmer for a few more minutes.

Now finish the sauce. Spoon a little of the cooking liquid into the blood to warm it up. Away from the heat, stir it into the sauce until well blended, return to the heat and simmer briskly for 1 minute, stirring all the time – the sauce should be a smooth, dark brown. If you reheat the dish, it will taste just as good though the sauce won't look quite as appealing since it tends to separate. Serve with croutons, if you like.

BLANQUETTE DE VEAU
Veal in a Cream and Mushroom Sauce

A CLASSIC OF BOURGEOIS COOKING AND quite rightly so. Delicate *blanquette* is a dish that does not like to be rushed. After years of producing not unpalatable concoctions that were the colour of milky coffee – unkindly called *brunettes* by the family – I adopted a gentler and more patient approach and, lo, my *blanquettes* turned a grateful shade of white.

Cook *blanquettes* on a day you want to relax in your kitchen and serve it with good plain rice and a bowl of small gherkins.

1.2 kg breast of veal	Serves 6 to 8	150 g button onions
1 carrot		1½ large lemons
1 large white Spanish onion		150 g button mushrooms
several sprigs each of thyme		45 g butter
and parsley		30 g flour
2 bay leaves	sea salt	1 or 2 large egg yolks
300 ml dry white wine	freshly ground black pepper	120 ml *crème fraîche*

TRIM THE BREAST OF VEAL, DISCARDING fat and sinew as necessary and cut into 4-cm pieces. Soak overnight or for several hours in plenty of fresh cold water. Once the veal has had a good soaking, peel the carrot and cut it into 4 chunks. Quarter the onion. Put the herbs and bay leaves on a small piece of muslin, make into a bag and tie with a string. Drain the veal.

Put the veal with the vegetables and muslin bag in a large, heavy-based saucepan. Pour in the wine and add just enough cold water to cover. Over a very moderate heat, bring slowly to a low boil. Conscientiously skim off any scum that may come up to the surface. Season lightly with salt and freshly ground black pepper. Reduce the heat a little and simmer *very* gently for 1¼ to 1½ hours, skimming whenever necessary. The meat should feel tender when you pierce it with a fork at the end of cooking.

Meanwhile, peel the button onions and blanch for 5 minutes in lightly salted water. Squeeze the lemons. Trim and slice the mushrooms and blanch well in boiling water with a dash of lemon juice for a couple of minutes. Drain the onions and mushrooms.

Strain the stock out of the pan into a bowl or jug, leaving the veal in the pan. Discard the muslin bag, then add the drained onions and mushrooms to the pan. Sprinkle with a little lemon juice and then cover to keep warm. If you want to cook the dish in stages, this is a good time to break off; allow a good 30 minutes to finish off later. And do make sure you reheat everything gently.

Melt the butter in a saucepan. Add the flour and stir for 1 minute to make a very pale roux – do not let it colour. Pour the hot stock into the roux and bring to the boil, stirring vigorously. Simmer gently for a good 10 to 15 minutes, stirring frequently, until the sauce is smooth and thickened. Now beat the egg yolk or yolks in a bowl, stir in a little hot sauce, then the *crème fraîche* and beat until thoroughly combined. Pour the mixture into the saucepan and stir over a low heat; do not boil.

Pour the sauce over the veal and vegetables. Return to a low heat and stir carefully for a couple of minutes until heated through. Sprinkle in the rest of the lemon juice, check the seasoning, stir and serve immediately.

Veau aux Girolles
Veal with Wild Mushrooms

Make this old-fashioned dish with the best mushrooms you think you can afford. I must admit that I only use little yellow horn-shaped *girolles* (also called *chanterelles*) if I have been lucky enough to be able to gather my own. Otherwise, I use small brown ones. I only buy wild mushrooms to enjoy them on their own, fried in the pan with a little butter, a hint of garlic and plenty of chopped parsley.

Serves 6

1.2 kg tender veal from the
    shoulder or leg, tied to make
    a neat joint
4 baby carrots
4 shallots
2 cloves of garlic
3 tablespoons olive oil
60 g butter, plus extra to finish
250 ml medium-sweet white
    wine
sea salt
freshly ground black pepper
750 g *girolles* or other fragrant
    mushrooms
2 tablespoons fresh
    breadcrumbs
a few sprigs of parsley and
    chervil

Wipe and slice the carrots. Finely chop the shallots and crush the garlic. Heat 1 tablespoon of oil and a good knob of butter in a flameproof casserole or sauté pan. Sauté the carrots, shallots and garlic for 1 minute over a very moderate heat, then add the veal joint and sauté until it looks evenly coloured, turning it over gradually.

Moisten the veal with half the wine and a similar amount of water. Season lightly with salt and freshly ground black pepper, then cover tightly.

Reduce the heat and cook very slowly for a good hour. Leave the meat to cool and relax a little. Heat the oven to 200°C/Gas 6.

Meanwhile, trim and wipe the mushrooms. Heat the rest of the oil in a large frying pan with a knob of butter. Add the mushrooms and let them sweat for a few minutes over a moderate heat, frequently shaking the pan. Season them with salt and freshly ground black pepper, then drain on paper towels. Cut the veal into thin slices. Spread half the mushrooms in a gratin dish. Arrange the slices of veal on top of the mushrooms.

Pour the rest of the wine into the casserole or sauté pan. Stir over a moderately high heat for a minute or two, scraping the bottom of the pan. Strain the pan juices over the veal. Cover with the rest of the mushrooms and sprinkle with the breadcrumbs. Snip the herbs over the breadcrumbs, then dot with the rest of the butter. Finish the dish in the oven for 5 minutes, until golden. Serve immediately.

CÔTES DE PORC AU CIDRE ET À L'OIGNON

Pan-Fried Pork Chops with Onion and Vinegar

A GOOD PAN-FRY to serve with sautéed apple slices, mashed potatoes or *gratin dauphinois* (see page 122).

Serves 4

4 pork chops, not too lean and cut fairly thick
1 clove of garlic
a few sprigs of thyme
4 sage leaves
freshly ground black pepper

4 tablespoons medium dry cider or white wine
1 small onion
1 shallot
olive oil, if needed

3 tablespoons cider or white wine vinegar
3 tablespoons single cream
2 teaspoons mild Dijon mustard
sea salt

CUT THE GARLIC AND RUB THE CHOPS well with the cut sides of the garlic. Snip the thyme and sage leaves over the chops, then sprinkle with freshly ground black pepper; rub this seasoning well in on both sides. Cover with plastic wrap and set aside at room temperature for about 1 hour.

Slit the fat around the chops at 2.5-cm intervals. Heat a sauté pan and put the chops in the pan. Cook them over a moderately high heat on both sides for a few minutes, until they turn brown and some fat runs out, then reduce the heat, moisten with the wine or cider and the same amount of water. Cover and cook very gently for 15 to 20 minutes. Remove the chops from the pan with tongs or a fish slice and keep them warm on a heated serving dish under a heated plate.

Meanwhile, chop the onion and shallot finely. If the chops haven't released much fat, add a little olive oil to the pan juices. Soften the onion and shallot for a few minutes over a moderate heat, stirring frequently. Add the vinegar, scrape the bottom of the pan well and bring to a simmer. Stir in the cream and mustard until hot. Season to taste with salt and a little extra pepper and spoon the sauce over the chops. Serve immediately.

Porc à la Boulangère
Roast Pork with Potatoes

A WEEKEND ROAST after my own heart. Any leftovers will be delicious served with a little garlicky mayonnaise. Use the same method with a leg or shoulder of lamb; it will work just as well.

Serves 6

900 g waxy potatoes
1 large white Spanish onion
oil for greasing
a few sprigs each of parsley
    and thyme

sea salt
freshly ground black pepper
300 ml chicken stock (see page
    12), light beef stock or water

60 g butter
1.5 kg loin of pork, boned,
    trimmed and tied
2 or 3 cloves of garlic
4 sage leaves

HEAT THE OVEN TO 170°C/GAS 3. PEEL and slice the potatoes fairly thickly. Thinly slice the onion. Grease a large gratin dish. Spread the sliced potatoes and onion over the bottom of the dish. Snip in the fresh herbs and season lightly with salt and freshly ground black pepper. Pour in just enough stock or water to cover the vegetables. Dot generously with butter and cover with foil. Cook in the oven for about 1 hour.

Now prepare the loin of pork. Cut the garlic and sage leaves into slivers. Using the point of a small, sharp knife, make several deep slits into the pork fat and insert the slivers of garlic and sage well into the slits. Rub the loin of pork with a little salt and more generously with freshly ground black pepper. Set aside at room temperature for about 40 minutes.

Very lightly grease the bottom of a sauté pan. Heat the pan and brown the pork lightly and evenly on all sides over a moderately high heat. Take the potatoes out of the oven, uncover and place the pork on top of the potatoes, replacing the foil before returning to the oven. Turn up the heat to 190°C/Gas 5 and cook for 1¼ to 1½ hours, until the pork is tender and cooked through. Remove the foil for the last 15 minutes.

This dish is best served simply. Leave the pork to relax for a few minutes, then remove it from the potatoes, cut into thin slices and arrange the slices, overlapping slightly, back on top of the potatoes.

CASSOULET MAISON
Pork and Haricot Bean Casserole

THIS RECIPE IS RELAXED, less fatty than most – and likely to be frowned on by *cassoulet* purists, since I include tomatoes. As I understand it, *cassoulet* is a flexible feast. One ingredient that cannot be left out is the *confit* (available from good gourmet delicatessens) with its inimitable fat and filamentous texture. Best prepared a day or two ahead, *cassoulet* makes a splendid *pièce de résistance* for a winter party. Drink with Cahors or Fitou wine. Mop up the juices with good bread and follow with heaps of sharpish green salad.

Serves 12

1 kg small white haricot beans
2 large bouquets garnis
2 large onions – 1 stuck with a few cloves
1 large carrot
225-g piece cured ham or smoked belly of pork
18 cloves of garlic, 12 unpeeled, the rest peeled
12 black peppercorns
225 g thick-cut smoked bacon

450-g can goose or duck *confit*
450 g canned tomatoes
600 ml good strong stock
a few sprigs of thyme

1 tablespoon strong Dijon mustard (optional)
few drops of chilli or Worcestershire sauce (definitely optional)
small glass of brandy (optional)
12 spicy country sausages (Toulouse or Cumberland)
a small bunch of parsley
90 g white breadcrumbs made from day-old bread

SOAK THE HARICOT BEANS IN PLENTY OF cold water for at least 6 hours. Drain, rinse and bring to the boil in plenty of fresh cold water, with 1 bouquet garni, the clove-studded onion, carrot, piece of ham or smoked belly of pork, 12 unpeeled garlic cloves and the peppercorns.

Reduce the heat and simmer gently, half-covered, for about 1½ hours until the beans are cooked but still a little firm.

Meanwhile, chop the remaining onion and garlic and the smoked bacon. In a large, heavy-based casserole, brown the onion in a little of the goose or duck fat from the *confit*. Skin the meat and cut into small pieces. Stir the pieces into the browned onion with the chopped bacon and garlic; discard the skin. Add the bones to the bean mixture. Cook for a few minutes, stirring, then pour in the tomatoes with their juice and the stock. Add the second bouquet garni, the thyme and any optional extras. Stir, cover and cook gently for 20 to 30 minutes.

Very slowly grill the sausages until crisp all over and cooked through, then cut into fork-size chunks.

Now, to assemble the *cassoulet*. Drain the beans and discard the onion, bones, bouquets garnis and peppercorns. Chop up the carrot and ham or pork (discarding the fat). If you are going to serve the *cassoulet* in the casserole, transfer the meat stew to a bowl. Ladle a good layer of beans into the casserole. Add half the carrot and ham or pork, then half the meat stew. Repeat the process, stretching the meat stew with extra hot water if it looks too thick and dry. Top with the remaining beans and the sausages. The *cassoulet* can be put aside at this stage, for up to 24 hours in a cool place.

To finish, snip the parsley into a bowl. Sprinkle the *cassoulet* with the breadcrumbs and parsley, then dot with some of the remaining duck/goose *confit*. About 45 to 60 minutes before serving, heat the oven to 200°C/Gas 6. Cover the *cassoulet* and heat for 20 minutes, then remove the lid and allow to brown for 20 minutes more. Serve very hot.

GIGOT
Leg of Lamb

ONE WORD OF CAUTION: you may be disappointed, but I am not going to offer a proper recipe for the greatest of all French festive meat dishes. *Gigot* has to be boldly cooked; there can be few adjustments and no camouflage. And the list of variables to be taken into consideration is more daunting than usual. First there is the lamb itself and the way it is butchered and prepared. Then comes the roasting tin or dish and the oven with its own little quirks and tricks. Last but not least, we have the cook, the carver and the guests, with their different hands and palates. And when *gigot* is at stake, in my experience, people always have strong views and great expectations. Quite rightly so. After all, *gigot* is the food of high days and holidays.

I HAVE EATEN OTHER PEOPLE'S PERFECT *gigot* and made a quiet note of it. I have on occasion achieved my idea of *gigot* bliss, only to be met by barely polite noises around my table. So rather than a recipe, let me tell you what works for me.

In an ideal world, I will use young Welsh or English lamb, butchered and trimmed French-style, studded with lots of garlic, well seasoned and rubbed with rosemary and thyme. I would have discussed the meat with my butcher, then decided whether or not to sit the *gigot* on a few good knobs of butter.

Before I put my *gigot* in the hot oven, I would dribble a little olive oil over it, then cook it very fast, basting a few times with the juices and a trickle of white wine.

Meanwhile, I would plead with the rest of the family, who like their lamb ultra-pink, for the *gigot* to be granted an extra few minutes in the oven and, hopefully, for injury time afterwards to relax. In the end I would serve it with *haricots verts* (see page 128), young flageolets (see page 129) and garlic sauce. And for these three items at least I can certainly provide recipes.

SAUCE À L'AIL
Garlic Sauce

DON'T BE PUT OFF by the 225 g garlic I use in this recipe. It is not a printing error and this easy-to-prepare sauce is more aromatic than pungent, because the garlic will be boiled three times. You'll also find that peeling the cooked cloves is a real cinch: simply squeeze them between your thumb and forefinger and they'll just pop out.

| 225 g cloves of garlic | Serves 6 | sea salt |
| 300 ml single cream | | freshly ground black pepper |

IN A MEDIUM-SIZE SAUCEPAN FILLED WITH plenty of cold water, bring the cloves of garlic to the boil.

As soon as the water starts bubbling, drain the cloves. Then return them to the pan, cover with fresh cold water and bring to the boil again. Drain, then repeat the process one more time.

Now squeeze the softened cloves (see above). Combine the cream and the peeled cloves in the saucepan and heat through gently until piping hot but not boiling, stirring occasionally. Purée the mixture, season with a little salt and more generously with freshly ground black pepper and serve with *gigot*. This sauce can be reheated if necessary.

Agneau en Papillote
Marinated Lamb in Foil

A RECIPE I HAVE USED and liked for years, from I-am-not-quite sure where in Provence. I serve this dish with rice, pasta and tomatoes wilted in a low oven for 1 hour with Mediterranean herbs and a pinch of sugar, or with tiny young flageolets (see page 129) when they are around.

	Serves 4	
900 g boned shoulder of lamb		a few fennel seeds
1 large ripe tomato		1 bay leaf
1 large unwaxed lemon	a couple of sprigs each of	a few mint leaves
75 ml virgin olive oil	thyme, marjoram, oregano	freshly ground black pepper
	and rosemary	sea salt

MODÈLE DÉPOSÉ EXCLUSIF A L'IMPRIMEUR ÉDITEUR

HUILE

1ʳᵉ Qualité **COMESTIBLE**

N° 553

TRIM THE FAT OFF THE MEAT, THEN CUT the shoulder into 12 pieces, not too small but no larger than 4 cm. Blanch the tomato in boiling water, then skin and remove the seeds and pulp and chop the flesh. Grate and squeeze the lemon.

In a soup plate or shallow bowl, combine the olive oil with the chopped tomato and the grated zest and juice of the lemon. Snip in the herbs. Add a few fennel seeds, then snip in the bay leaf and the mint leaves. Season with freshly ground black pepper. Carefully roll the pieces of lamb in this marinade until they are coated all over. Cover and leave to marinate for 2 hours at room temperature, or longer in the refrigerator.

Heat the oven to 220°C/Gas 7 with a baking tray in it. Cut 4 squares of foil, each large enough to comfortably wrap around 3 pieces of lamb. Put 3 pieces of marinated lamb in the centre of each square of foil. Spoon any remaining marinade over the lamb. Season with a little salt and extra pepper. Close the packages, but not too tightly. Put them on the hot baking tray.

Cook for 20 to 25 minutes and leave the meat to settle for 10 minutes before you open the foil packages.

Navarin d'Agneau
Lamb Stew with Turnips

A TRUSTED LAMB STEW. Feel free to vary the vegetables. The turnips are a traditional ingredient, but I sometimes replace them with potatoes, then add leeks and tomatoes halfway through the cooking.

1 kg boned lamb shoulder or
  chump
freshly ground black pepper
1 large white Spanish onion
225 g carrots
450 g turnips
2 or 3 cloves of garlic
1 tablespoon oil

Serves 6

2 teaspoons flour
300 ml light beef stock or water
90 ml dry white wine
several sprigs of parsley and
  rosemary
sea salt
15 g butter or 1 tablespoon
  cream, to finish, if liked

TRIM A GOOD DEAL OF THE VISIBLE FAT from the meat. Cut it into 5-cm pieces. Sprinkle the pieces with finely ground black pepper and set aside while you prepare the vegetables. Coarsely chop the onion; trim and peel the carrots and the turnips. Cut into chunks; crush the garlic.

Heat the oil in a casserole or large sauté pan. Over a moderately high heat, sauté the meat until lightly coloured, then add the vegetables and sauté for a few minutes, stirring frequently. Sprinkle the flour over the dish and stir to mix it in. Then pour in the stock and the white wine.

Bring the liquid to a simmer, then snip in the herbs and season with salt and freshly ground black pepper. Cover, reduce the heat and cook for about 1½ hours. Skim off the surface fat and scum occasionally.

Once the stew is cooked, remove the meat and vegetables from the pot with a draining spoon; keep them warm. Skim off any fat, then strain the liquid and return it to the pot, turn up the heat and reduce a little. Check the seasoning. Swirl in a knob of butter or a spoonful of cream, if you wish, then return the meat and vegetables to the pot, stir them in well and serve immediately.

Tagine de Mouton Yonnée
Pot-Roasted Lamb with Onions and Raisins

THE PAST IS ANOTHER COUNTRY and like everyone else I have always been intrigued by my parents' past, the remote land of before my time. My father and his brothers spent a few happy years as children in North Africa. He returned during the war after escaping from a German POW camp. There he met up with his brother, Jean and sister-in-law, Yonnée. They were all actively working for the Free French. These were dangerous but exciting days and I have never tired of hearing about them. Many of the North African stories were told around a *couscous* or *tagine* and over a glass of Boulaouane greyish rosé wine. This recipe of my aunt's is as simple as it is delectable and should be served with rice.

Serves 6

45 g raisins
250 ml of cold weak tea
1.2 to 1.4 kg shoulder of
    mature lamb
3 tablespoons olive oil
2½ large unwaxed lemons
1 good pinch of powdered
    saffron
1 tablespoon powdered cumin
3 cloves of garlic
sea salt
freshly ground black pepper
900 g large white Spanish
    onions

SOAK THE RAISINS IN WEAK TEA overnight or for several hours. Trim most of the visible fat from the lamb, then cut it into 5-cm pieces.

Grease a flameproof casserole with a little olive oil. Grate and squeeze 1 lemon. Put the meat pieces in the casserole, then sprinkle in the lemon juice and zest, the saffron and the cumin. Add the garlic. Chop up another lemon and add it. Season lightly with salt and freshly ground black pepper. Cover and very slowly cook over an extremely low heat for 3 hours.

After about 2½ hours, thinly slice the onions. Heat the rest of the olive oil in a sauté pan and very gently sweat and cook the onions. Stir them frequently and do not let them turn brown. Drain the raisins. When the onions are nearly done, stir in the drained raisins.

Add the onions and raisins to the lamb, stir and cook together for a few minutes. Squeeze the remaining half lemon and sprinkle the juice over the dish. Stir and check the seasoning. This dish should be served piping hot.

ROGNONS AU VIN ROUGE
Kidneys in Red Wine

A QUICK AND tasty dish that is good with plain rice.

450 g lamb's kidneys	Serves 4	freshly ground black pepper
3 shallots		grated nutmeg
1 clove of garlic		2 teaspoons flour
1 tablespoon oil		2 teaspoons mild Dijon
30 g butter		mustard
120 ml red wine		2 tablespoons double cream
1 bay leaf		several sprigs of fresh parsley
sea salt		

MAKE THE SAUCE. FINELY CHOP THE shallots and garlic. Heat half the oil and a good knob of butter in a heavy-based saucepan. Sweat the shallots and garlic over a low heat until soft, without allowing them to colour. Pour in the red wine and 3 tablespoons of cold water. Add the bay leaf and simmer gently for 5 minutes, stirring occasionally.

Finally, season with a little salt, freshly ground black pepper and a small pinch of grated nutmeg.

While the sauce is cooking, prepare the kidneys. Rinse them well under cold running water, then pat dry with paper towels and trim off any skin and core. Cut each kidney in half lengthways. Melt the rest of the butter in a frying pan. Dust the kidneys with flour, then sauté them over a moderately high heat for 3 to 4 minutes on each side, until they stiffen a little and change colour.

Remove the kidneys from the pan with a draining spoon and keep warm.

Pour the sauce into the frying pan and stir it in thoroughly, scraping up the pan sediments. Add the mustard and the cream and stir in well, then return the kidneys and their juices to the pan. Stir until heated through.

Snip the parsley and sprinkle over the kidneys. To enjoy this dish at its peak, serve immediately.

BŒUF BOURGUIGNON
Beef Cooked in Red Burgundy

SINCE THIS DISH is infinitely better reheated, I always make it the day before. The last-minute addition of brandy, wine and butter brings the *bourguignon* alive and literally makes the sauce shine.

	Serves 4	
900 g chuck or blade steak		1 bottle Burgundy or similar
2 thick-cut slices smoked		style wine
bacon		sea salt
1 large white Spanish onion		freshly ground black pepper
1 clove of garlic		1 tablespoon brandy
1 tablespoon oil	a few sprigs of thyme	30 g butter
1 tablespoon flour	1 bay leaf	several sprigs of fresh parsley

PREFERABLY START COOKING THE DISH ON the day before you intend to eat it. Trim any surplus fat off the beef. Cut the meat into chunks, not bigger than 5 cm square. Chop the bacon and onion and crush the garlic. Heat the oil in a flameproof casserole or large sauté pan. Sauté the bacon until it turns brown. Turn up the heat a bit, add the beef and brown quickly on all sides.

Remove the meat from the pan with a draining spoon. Add the onion and sauté until it colours. Return the meat to the pan, add the garlic and sprinkle with the flour. Stir for a few minutes, then add the thyme, bay leaf and three-quarters of the wine. Season with salt, more generously with freshly ground black pepper and bring to a simmer, stirring occasionally.

Now reduce the heat to very low, cover tightly and cook extremely slowly for at least 2½ hours, giving the mixture an occasional stir. Turn off the heat and leave overnight to mature.

The next day, very gently reheat the dish for about 40 minutes. Carefully take out the meat with tongs or a draining spoon and put it on a plate, or if you prefer, pile it on a serving dish. Then turn up the heat a little, stir in the brandy and continue to cook for a few minutes.

Meanwhile, snip the parsley. Pour the rest of the wine into the pan, swirl in the butter and stir, then either return the meat to the pan or pour the sauce over the meat in the serving dish. Sprinkle with the parsley and serve immediately.

Bœuf en Daube
Slow-Cooked Beef Casserole

ONE OF MY FAVOURITE French country casseroles and very different in texture and flavour. Unlike *bœuf bourguignon*, this dish is best served with rice or pasta rather than potatoes.

1 kg braising steak	**Serves 5 or 6**	2 cloves of garlic
1 large white Spanish onion		2 large ripe tomatoes
1 shallot		12 black olives
2 bay leaves	3 tablespoons olive oil	200 g mushrooms
several sprigs each of thyme	550 ml light red or white wine	sea salt
and parsley	4 thick-cut slices of smoked	freshly ground black pepper
a few black peppercorns	bacon	

TRIM ANY VISIBLE FAT OFF THE MEAT, then cut into 5-cm chunks. Chop the onion and shallot. In a large bowl, combine the meat, onion, shallot, bay leaves, thyme, parsley and peppercorns with half the oil and just enough red wine to cover. Leave to marinate overnight.

The next day, heat the oven to 170°C/Gas 3. Chop the bacon. In a flameproof casserole, heat the rest of the oil. Add the bacon and sauté until it begins to brown. Take the meat out of the marinade, reserving the marinade. Drain the meat well and pat dry with a clean cloth or paper towels. Add the meat to the dish and brown on all sides for a few minutes over a moderately high heat.

Coarsely chop the garlic and tomatoes. Stone and chop the olives, and wipe and slice the mushrooms. Add all these to the dish together with the onion and shallot from the marinade; stir well.

Cover the dish tightly and cook in the oven for 20 minutes.

Take the dish out of the oven and pour in the reserved marinade. Season to taste with salt and freshly ground black pepper. Stir thoroughly, cover the dish tightly again and return to the oven.

Turn the oven down to 130°C/Gas ½. Cook for a good 3 hours, occasionally checking to see that there is still enough wine to come halfway up the pieces of meat. Add a little extra wine if necessary. Serve hot. Leftovers are delicious cold.

Pot au Feu
Boiled Beef with Vegetables

THE GRAND OLD one-pot meal of France – and a good way to make a proper light beef stock. In my experience, there is never a great deal of left-over beef, but what there may be is excellent served cold with a garlicky mayonnaise.
There never seems to be enough marrow either. When I was a child, the precious substance was always ceremoniously given on a piece of toast to my grandmother, while we all wondered what on earth the fuss was about.

Serves 8

1 kg lean braising beef
1 kg shin of beef, meat and
   bone
1 large marrow bone
3 cloves of garlic
2 bay leaves
several sprigs of thyme
6 carrots
4 turnips
4 medium-size potatoes

8 button onions
4 large leeks
4 stalks of celery
sea salt

several sprigs each of chervil
   and parsley
freshly ground black pepper

TO SERVE
strong Dijon mustard
coarse-grain mustard
coarse kosher salt
gherkins
creamed horseradish

INTO YOUR LARGEST, HEAVY-BASED saucepan or stockpot, put the meat bones. Trim off most of the visible fat, then cut the meat into large pieces – no smaller than about 7.5 cm square – and tie them together. Put the meat on top of the bones. Cover with plenty of cold water, add the garlic, bay leaves and thyme and very slowly bring to the boil over an extremely low heat. Skim off any greyish scum as soon as it comes up to the surface.

While the meat is coming to the boil, carefully prepare the vegetables. Peel the carrots and cut them into segments. Peel the turnips and cut in half, or quarter them if they are large. Peel the potatoes and cut in half. Peel the onions neatly. Trim the leeks, cut in half lengthways and rinse them well. Trim and rinse the stalks of celery. Tie together the leeks and celery into 3 bundles.

Add the carrots, turnips and potatoes to the pan. Bring back to a very gentle boil and skim off any scum. Season lightly with salt. Now add the onions and the leek and celery

bundles. Bring back to a low boil, skim again and partly cover. Cook very slowly for at least another 2½ hours, skimming until any foam that comes up looks light and white. Add the parsley and chervil after about 1 hour of cooking.

Remove from the heat and leave to settle for a few minutes. Remove any surface fat with a spoon. Lift out the meat and vegetables with a draining spoon. Discard the strings, then heap meat and vegetables attractively on a serving dish. Spoon out the marrow and reserve for your most honoured or senior guest; discard the bones.

Strain the stock through a strainer lined with muslin or a clean fine cloth into a saucepan. Bring to a simmer, add a little freshly ground black pepper and salt, if necessary, and moisten the meat and vegetables with a little sauce. Pour some more stock into a bowl to serve with the dish. Have on the table at the same time different kinds of mustards, coarse salt and creamed horseradish.

BŒUF MODE
Braised Beef

BŒUF MODE CAN BE SERVED hot or cold, which I much prefer. It makes a splendid party dish.

Serves 8

1 calf's foot, split in half	300 ml dry white wine, plus extra, if needed	2 or 3 bay leaves
4 thick-cut slices of smoked back bacon	2 cloves of garlic	sea salt
1.8 kg rolled topside of beef, larded and barded	several sprigs of parsley and thyme	freshly ground black pepper about 24 button onions 450 g baby carrots

RINSE AND SCRUB THE CALF'S FOOT, THEN blanch it for a few minutes in boiling water. Drain the foot and, if you wish and possess a cleaver or heavy knife, cut into pieces. Chop the bacon.

Place a large flameproof casserole over a moderate heat. Add the chopped bacon to the pot and sauté until the juices begin to run. Add the beef and brown lightly and evenly on all sides. Now add the calf's foot and moisten with the white wine and about the same quantity of water. Chop or crush the garlic and add to the dish with the sprigs of herbs and the bay leaves. Season lightly with salt and freshly ground black pepper. Cover tightly and cook over a very low heat for a good 2 hours.

After about 2 hours, peel and trim the onions. Scrape the baby carrots and cut into segments. Add the onions and carrots to the pan with a little extra wine and water if the level of the liquid looks too low. Cover and cook for 1½ hours more over a low heat.

If you want to eat this dish hot, leave the pot off the heat for at least 10 minutes and skim the fat off the surface before serving. Chill any remains: the jellied leftovers will be excellent served cold the following day.

To serve the whole dish cold, allow the beef to cool in the pot until barely warm. Remove it from the pot and leave to get cold on a large plate, then cover it with foil and chill for a couple of hours. Strain the liquid, reserving the vegetables and the pieces of calf's foot. Leave the liquid to get cold and then chill. Also refrigerate the vegetables and calf's foot.

Remove the strings and the outer fat from the chilled beef and cut it into thin slices. Arrange the slices on a large serving dish, so they overlap. Surround with the reserved vegetables and pieces of calf's foot. Spoon the jellied or syrupy sauce over the dish and sprinkle very lightly with freshly ground black pepper. Cover the dish with plastic wrap or foil and chill until ready to serve.

STEAKS AU POIVRE ET AUX ANCHOIS
Steaks with Pepper and Anchovy

ONE OF MY FAVOURITE 'quickie' sauces. My husband is more a steak-eater than I and he believes in warming the steaks in a little butter before patting in the crushed peppercorns. It does seem to deepen the peppery flavour, but since Colin got the idea from a James Beard book I am only mentioning this as an aside and for the sake of *entente cordiale* and *matrimoniale*.

Serves 4

4 steaks, from the fillet or
   rump, about 4 cm thick
2 level tablespoons black
   peppercorns
1 tablespoon oil
60 g butter
2 tablespoons dry white wine
3 tablespoons *crème fraîche* or
   double cream
2 teaspoons anchovy paste
1 tablespoon brandy

AT LEAST 1 HOUR BEFORE YOU WANT TO start cooking the steaks, crush the peppercorns with the help of a mortar and pestle. Sprinkle the crushed peppercorns over the steaks, then press them in firmly with your hands. Cover with plastic wrap and set aside at room temperature.

Meanwhile, in a large, heavy-based frying pan, heat the oil and a good knob of butter over a high heat. Cut the rest of the butter into small pieces. Then add the steaks and cook them for 2 to 4 minutes on each side,

depending on your taste and the thickness and cut of the meat.

Put the steaks on a hot serving dish. Now swirl the wine into the pan, stir it for a minute, scraping the bottom of the pan, then add the cream and anchovy paste. Stir the sauce until it is heated through and swirl in the brandy.

Away from the heat, swirl in the pieces of chopped-up butter. Then pour the sauce over the steaks on their serving dish and serve at once.

HACHIS PARMENTIER
French Cottage Pie

THERE IS ABSOLUTELY no reason to turn up one's nose (however refined) at left-over beef when it is done this way. Having said that, I must admit that bland *hachis parmentier*, thriftily made from plain ground cooked beef and thin potato purée, is a pretty mean-spirited concoction. The one we did at home wasn't particularly economical, but it did taste good. And very often I much preferred it to the roast it originated from.

2 thick-cut slices of smoked bacon 1 smallish onion 2 shallots 1 clove of garlic 1 tablespoon olive oil 60 g butter about 350 g cooked beef	**Serves 4 or 5** 4 tablespoons red wine sea salt freshly ground black pepper a pinch of cayenne pepper or chilli powder, if liked	a dash of Worcestershire sauce a dash of tomato ketchup about 350 g not too heavy *purée de pommes de terre* (see page 123) 45 g Gruyère cheese 3 tablespoons breadcrumbs made from day-old bread

BRIEFLY WHIZZ TOGETHER THE BACON, onion, shallots and garlic in a food processor. Heat the oil with a knob of butter in a frying pan. Brown the bacon, onion and garlic mixture over a fairly high heat. Meanwhile, quickly process the cooked beef. Add the beef to the pan, stir it in well and sauté for a couple of minutes, still over a fairly high heat. Heat the oven to 230°C/Gas 8. Pour the wine into the frying pan and season to taste with salt and freshly ground black pepper. Add a little cayenne or chilli, if liked, and a dash of Worcestershire sauce and the ketchup. Reduce the heat a little and simmer for 10 minutes, stirring occasionally.

Butter a gratin dish. Spread a thin layer of creamed potato over the bottom of the dish. Cover with an even layer of beef hash. Cover with the rest of the potato. Grate the Gruyère over the dish and sprinkle with the breadcrumbs. Then dot with the rest of the butter. Bake the *hachis* for 15 minutes, until the topping is golden brown. Serve immediately.

LÉGUMES
Vegetables

WHENEVER THEY COME back from a holiday in France, my English and American vegetarian friends are always quick to point out that they find eating in the average French restaurant rather a depressing experience.

They explain vividly that there are very few vegetables on menus – never mind vegetarian dishes. I make patriotic excuses, of course, but to some extent I sympathise with them. A couple of year ago, travelling around the Toulouse–Albi region and eating in restaurants that the locals treated as their canteens, I soon wondered where all the vegetables were. This was September and the markets were bursting with vivid colours and mellow produce. But here we were, everywhere we went, being offered five-course menus that were incredibly high on value and animal protein. Withdrawal symptoms soon set in and I got to munching tomatoes in the car. After a few days, when we got to Cahors, I was overwhelmed with joy to discover that it had one vegetarian restaurant. It was tucked away near the cathedral, a throwback to the Seventies in its treatment of nut rissoles and general décor. But, how wonderful, at last, to be able to savour a meal built on the wealth of vegetables I had admired at the markets.

To eat vegetables in France, you have to go to someone's home. Depending on whether it is lunch or dinner, you'll begin the meal with crudités or soup, probably have potatoes or maybe plain rice or pasta with the main course, then almost certainly a green salad. A separate vegetable course is a strong possibility in the evening, particularly if the meal does not include meat. In fact, provided they eat eggs as well, I think my vegetarian friends would very much enjoy supper in a French home.

Ratatouille
Ragout of Provençal Vegetables

Ratatouille TASTES BEST in late summer when vegetables are at their peak of ripeness. There is a painstaking way of making *ratatouille*, which involves sautéing the vegetables separately before the final assembly. It produces an excellent *ratatouille*, but it takes infinitely longer than the recipe below. And somehow I don't think the end result justifies the effort. I prefer this slightly coarser version. If nothing else, it is closer in spirit to the name of the dish: *touiller* is a slangy way of saying stir or mix. As for *rata*, any French conscript will tell you that it just means plain old army grub.

Ratatouille is particularly good served with a plain omelette.

Serves 4 to 6

2 medium-size aubergines
3 cloves of garlic
90 ml olive oil
2 red peppers
1 large white onion
6 small courgettes
2 large ripe tomatoes
a few sprigs of thyme, sweet
   savoury, marjoram and
   oregano
sea salt
freshly ground black pepper
several sprigs of parsley

PEEL THE AUBERGINES AND CUT THEM crossways into thin slices. Cut one of the cloves of garlic and use it to rub a wide heavy-based saucepan or sauté pan. Crush the rest of the garlic. Heat 2 tablespoons of olive oil in the pan. Sauté the sliced aubergines for a few minutes.

Meanwhile, core and thinly slice the peppers. Add the peppers to the pan and sauté gently for a few minutes, until softened; take care not to overcook them.

Slice the onion very thinly. Add another tablespoon of olive oil to the pan, then stir in the onion rings. Sauté for a few minutes, stirring occasionally.

Meanwhile, cut the courgettes, then blanch, peel, seed and chop the tomatoes. Stir the courgettes into the pan. Sauté for a couple of minutes, then add the chopped tomatoes and the crushed garlic. Snip in the thyme, sweet savoury, marjoram and oregano; season lightly with salt and freshly ground black pepper. Stir in another 2 tablespoons of olive oil and cover the pan. Reduce the heat a little and cook gently for 30 to 40 minutes, stirring occasionally.

Snip in the parsley and add 1 more tablespoon of olive oil. Continue cooking on a low heat for 5 to 10 minutes. Check the seasoning. Serve hot, warm or cold, as you prefer.

GRATIN DAUPHINOIS
Potato Gratin

DAUPHINOIS, THE GREATEST *GRATIN* of them all, is a traditional accompaniment to roasts. In my opinion, at its creamy luxurious best, it deserves to be a course in its own right.

Gratin dauphinois is another of those dishes that no two people will ever make exactly the same. Mado, my grandmother's cook, first taught me a *gratin* made with thick-cut potatoes, milk, no eggs and good knobs of butter. My mother preferred thick slices of potato, 2 eggs and a mixture of milk and *crème fraîche*. I now find that if I am using cream, the *gratin* works best with thin slices and if milk, thick slices . . . Ah well. One egg yolk does help though and the good thing is, you can't really go wrong anyway.

Serves 6 to 8

900 g large waxy potatoes
2 or 3 cloves of garlic
butter
550 ml full-fat milk, or 450 ml
    single cream, or a mixture of
    the two
1 egg yolk
a pinch of grated nutmeg
sea salt
freshly ground black pepper

HEAT THE OVEN TO 170°C/GAS 3. PEEL the potatoes and slice them evenly – I do this with the slicing disc of the food processor. Leave to drain in a colander for 5 to 10 minutes, patting dry with paper towels. Cut the cloves of garlic. Rub a gratin dish thoroughly with the cut sides of the cloves, then crush the garlic. Generously grease the dish with butter.

Gently warm the milk, cream or mixture of both in a saucepan. Whisk in the egg yolk and stir in a pinch of nutmeg. Season with a little salt and freshly ground black pepper.

Spread a layer of potatoes in the prepared dish. Scatter some of the crushed garlic over them and season lightly. Spoon or trickle in a little of the milk or cream mixture. Repeat until all the potatoes are used up, ending with a good layer of milk or cream. Dot the surface with several little knobs of butter.

Cook in the oven for 1 hour, then turn up the heat to 200°C/Gas 6 and cook for 20 to 30 minutes more, until the *gratin* is golden brown and the potatoes tender: this you can test with a skewer.

If the potatoes aren't quite done, reduce the heat to the original setting and cook for another 15 minutes.

PURÉE DE POMMES DE TERRE MARTHE
Creamed Potatoes

MARTHE WAS MY family's maid in Paris and was quite a character. She had left school at 12, but she wrote well-turned sentences in a fine hand and could be relied on to advise us on grammar. She wore dentures that fascinated us and she had a strange habit of piecing together torn-up letters from wastepaper baskets. One day she confronted my father with one such discarded message. She was livid. How *could* Monsieur . . . Monsieur had so hated the Camembert at supper the previous evening that he had written a sarcastic note to Marthe to that effect – he always left for work before she arrived. Naturally he had soon thought better of it and torn up the note. We girls sided with her. How could anyone be so cruel, even if he changed his mind later. Marthe made the best creamed potatoes I have ever tasted, deceptively light and totally irresistible. This is more or less her recipe – rather less than more, because I use a little less egg and butter.

1.1 kg floury potatoes sea salt 100 ml milk 1 tablespoon cream	**Serves 6 to 8**	60 g butter, plus extra to finish, if liked 1 egg yolk freshly ground black pepper

BRING A LARGE SAUCEPAN OF LIGHTLY salted water to the boil. Peel the potatoes and cut them in half, or quarters if they are very large. Add the potatoes to the boiling water and bring it back to the boil. Reduce the heat a little and simmer gently until the potatoes are cooked, but not mushy. Do not let the water bubble too fast, or the potatoes will cook unevenly and disintegrate.

Meanwhile, heat the milk in a small saucepan until very hot, but not quite boiling; drain the potatoes well. Pass them through a *mouli* or mash lightly with a potato masher. Return the potatoes to the pan, with the butter, and stir gently over a low heat to remove the excess moisture.

Whisk in half the hot milk, then the cream, working vigorously. Beat the egg into the last few spoonfuls of milk and whisk this into the potatoes; season to taste. If you like, swirl in a good knob of butter. Serve at once.

The purée should not really be reheated (except when making *hachis parmentier*, page 119). But it will keep warm for up to 15 minutes in a bowl, covered with a heated plate, set over a pan of very hot water.

Pommes de Terre Sautées
Tata Boucher

Sautéed Potatoes

I HAVE ALREADY mentioned Madame Boucher, she of the magnificent omelettes. Her sautéed potatoes were equally satisfying. Perhaps this is why in our gratefulness we dubbed her Tata: although not our aunt or great-aunt, she was an honorary and honoured member of the family.

1 kg waxy potatoes
75 ml oil
45 g butter

Serves 6

sea salt
freshly ground black pepper
several sprigs of parsley

PEEL THE POTATOES AND CUT THEM INTO small dice, about 2 cm and certainly no larger than 1 inch. Rinse the diced potatoes in hot water, drain well and dry them thoroughly with a clean cloth or paper towels – this seems to prevent the potatoes from sticking together during cooking.

In a very large, heavy-based frying pan, heat the oil and butter. Add the potatoes – the pan should be large enough to take them very comfortably more or less in a single layer; otherwise use 2 pans.

Season liberally with salt and pepper. Over a low heat sauté the potatoes until crisp and golden: this may take up to 1 hour. Turn the heat down if the potatoes are browning too much. Stir frequently with a wooden spatula and give the pan an occasional good shake. Snip the parsley into a bowl and add the potatoes. They won't need draining but if they look even remotely greasy, drain them on paper towels. Check the seasoning and sprinkle the potatoes with extra snipped parsley. Serve hot.

Poireaux à la Crème

Leeks with Cream

THIS IS A GOOD VEGETABLE DISH to bear in mind if you know you are going to be pushed for time at the last minute. The softened leeks will happily keep for several hours. Reheat and finish off just before serving. Delicious with fish, particularly as a bed for seabass.

1 kg leeks
60 g butter
sea salt

Serves 6

freshly ground black pepper
2 to 3 tablespoons *crème fraîche*
or sour cream

TRIM THE LEEKS. SLIT THEM LENGTHWAYS and wash thoroughly in cold water. Drain well, dry with paper towels and chop. Melt the butter in a sauté pan, then stir in the leeks.

Cover and cook over a low heat until soft (20 minutes). Shake the pan often. Season with salt and freshly ground black pepper. Stir in the *crème fraîche* or sour cream. Serve hot.

Petits Pois à la Laitue et aux Petits Oignons
Baby Peas with Lettuce and Onions

FRESH FROM THE GARDEN, *petits pois* have always been one of the joys of the summer table. I sometimes add one or two chopped slices of unsmoked bacon to the other ingredients at the beginning of the recipe.

	Serves 4	
2 kg unshelled, or 500 g shelled baby peas		150 ml light chicken stock or water
60 g butter		1 teaspoon sugar
2 tender lettuces		sea salt
1 medium-sized mild onion, or 2 small onions		freshly ground black pepper

SHELL THE PEAS. MELT THE BUTTER IN A heavy-based saucepan. Wash and coarsely shred the lettuces. Peel and very thinly slice the onion or onions. Add the peas, lettuces and onion to the pan. Stir to coat in butter, then cover. Cook very gently over a low heat for 5 to 10 minutes, shaking the pan occasionally.

Add the stock or cold water and sprinkle in the sugar. Season with a little salt and freshly ground black pepper.

Cover and cook over a low heat for 10 to 15 minutes until the peas are tender. Taste and adjust the seasoning. Drain well and serve immediately.

Carottes au Cumin
Carrots Cooked with Cumin

A GOOD WAY to cook mature carrots.

	Serves 6	
1.2 kg carrots		freshly ground black pepper
2 to 3 tablespoons olive oil		1 or 2 cloves of garlic
1 teaspoon ground cumin		3 tablespoons white wine
sea salt		

PEEL AND SLICE THE CARROTS. HEAT THE oil in a sauté pan. Add the carrots and cumin, season lightly with salt and freshly ground black pepper and cook over a low heat for about 15 minutes, stirring occasionally.

Crush the garlic and add to the pan. Stir well, then moisten with the white wine and a glass of water. Cover and cook very gently for 45 minutes, shaking the pan from time to time. Drain and serve hot.

EMINCÉ DE CAROTTES ET DE COURGETTES
Sautéed Carrot and Courgette Ribbons

WATCHING COOKS GOING ABOUT their kitchen is the best way to learn. When I saw my sister Anne-Sophie Naudin prepare this pretty combination of faintly sweet, tender vegetables livened up by shallots and a splash of vermouth, I knew this was a dish I would do again and again – perfect for when you want something a bit special to serve with fish or white meat.

Serves 6

450 g carrots
450 g courgettes
1½ tablespoons olive oil
30 g butter
2 shallots

3 tablespoons Noilly-Prat, or other dry vermouth or dry sherry

1 tablespoon *crème fraîche*
2 tablespoons finely chopped parsley
sea salt and freshly ground black pepper

GRATE THE CARROTS AND COURGETTES, using a food mill or food processor. In a large frying pan, over a low heat, mix the oil with half the butter. Add the vegetables, season and cook over a low heat for 10 minutes, stirring from time to time.

Peel and finely chop the shallots. Add to the pan, stir in the rest of the butter and continue cooking and stirring occasionally for about 10 minutes until tender, keeping the heat low. Stir in the Noilly-Prat, cook for 2 minutes, then stir in the cream and parsley. Remove from the heat, adjust the seasoning and serve hot.

Gratin d'Aubergines
Aubergine Gratin

From the family's summer repertoire, a dish that seduced my elders on the island of Porquerolles, off the Lavandou coast, between Toulon and St Tropez. I often leave out the Gruyère to be able to enjoy the full Mediterranean flavours of the vegetables, but Gruyère featured in the original recipe and so stays in as an option. This is a good dish for vegetarians.

3 or 4 unblemished large, long aubergines	**Serves 6**	a few sprigs of marjoram and oregano
olive oil		1 to 2 teaspoons sugar
750 g ripe tomatoes		sea salt
2 or 3 cloves of garlic		freshly ground black pepper
several sprigs each of parsley, thyme and chervil		150 g Gruyère cheese, if liked

Wipe the aubergines. Slice them thinly lengthways without peeling. Heat 1 tablespoon of olive oil in a large frying pan. Sauté the aubergine slices over a moderate heat, a few at a time. Turn them over as soon as they become a little crisp and golden on the underside. Drain them well on a thick layer of paper towels, turning them over to mop up as much fat as possible.

Continue in the same way until all the aubergine slices have been sautéed, adding more oil as necessary. Turn down the heat a little after a while and resist any impulse to speed up the process – aubergines burn all too readily. At the same time blanch the tomatoes in boiling water, then peel them, cut in half, remove the seeds and chop the flesh coarsely.

Crush the garlic. In the sauté pan, heat 1 tablespoon of olive oil. Tip in the tomatoes. Add the crushed garlic, snip in the herbs and sprinkle in the sugar. Cook over a low heat until the mixture becomes a soft purée, stirring frequently. Season with a little salt and freshly ground black pepper. Heat the oven to 180°C/Gas 4. Grate the Gruyère, if using.

Put a layer of aubergine slices in the bottom of a gratin dish. Season lightly. Spread a thin layer of tomato purée over the aubergines. If you are using Gruyère, sprinkle a little on top of the tomatoes. Repeat until all the ingredients are used up. Sprinkle the top layer with a little olive oil. Cook in the oven for a good hour. Eat warm rather than hot and preferably as a separate course.

Purée d'Oignons
Onion Purée

THIS SIDE DISH nicely accompanies plain roasts, grills and pan-fries. It can be made well ahead and reheated at the last minute. I sometimes add a few cloves of garlic to the onions.

30 g raisins
200 ml hot weak tea
500 g onions
2 tablespoons sunflower or
    peanut oil
30 g sugar

Serves 6

90 ml dry white wine
3 tablespoons white wine
    vinegar
sea salt
freshly ground black pepper

SOAK THE RAISINS IN THE HOT WEAK TEA. Meanwhile, coarsely chop the onions. Heat the oil in a saucepan. Over a low heat, gently sweat the onions in the oil, without letting them brown. Sprinkle in the sugar, stir and cover. Reduce the heat to very low, cover and cook for 15 minutes, occasionally shaking the pan.

Now add the wine. Stir, cover and cook for another 15 minutes, still very gently. Stir in the vinegar and continue cooking for 10 minutes. Drain the raisins and add them to the pan as well, season lightly and cook for 15 minutes more. The onions will be meltingly soft and only lightly coloured. Serve hot.

Haricots Verts Fourchettes
French Beans

ON SUMMER EVENINGS, at my grandparents' house, supper often consisted of vast platters of beans prepared this way. The exact amount of butter, garlic and parsley varies with the cook. The quantities below are a moderate guideline.

500 g young thin green beans
sea salt
1 small clove of garlic

Serves 4

several sprigs of parsley
45 g butter
freshly ground black pepper

TOP AND TAIL THE BEANS AND REMOVE any strings. Bring a large saucepan of water to the boil and add a little salt. Throw in the beans, bring back to the boil and keep it that way until the beans are cooked to your liking, but preferably still a little firm. While the beans are cooking, crush the garlic and snip the parsley into a bowl.

Have a big bowl of ice water ready. Quickly drain the beans and plunge into the ice water. Leave them in for a few seconds and drain again. Dry in a clean cloth if you like. Now melt the butter in a sauté pan. Add the beans to the butter with the garlic and parsley. Mix well, stir over a moderate heat and serve when heated through.

FLAGEOLETS AU NATUREL
Simple Flageolet Beans

A DISH I ONLY DO when I see really attractive, fresh-looking small flageolets, sometimes at my local health-food store in London, but more likely on a French market stall in the autumn. The rest of the time I am content enough with my cans (see page 130).

Ideal with *gigot* and good with duck, these flageolets (without the butter finish) also make the basis of a good salad. Dress with extra-virgin olive oil and lemon juice, add plenty of snipped spring onions, chives, and parsley, then serve at room temperature.

500 g young flageolet beans	Serves 4 to 6	1.5 litres liquid made up from
a few sprigs each of thyme and		chicken stock and water
marjoram		sea salt
3 sage leaves		freshly ground black pepper
1 bay leaf		45 g butter
1 clove of garlic		several sprigs of fresh parsley

SOAK THE FLAGEOLETS FOR 1 TO 2 HOURS – the fresher they are, the less they will need to soak. Discard any damaged beans that come up to the surface; drain and rinse. Place the herbs and the garlic on a piece of muslin. Form the muslin into a little pouch and secure it with fine string. Into a large, heavy-based saucepan, pour the chicken stock and water. Add the flageolets and muslin pouch.

Bring slowly to the boil and skim off any scum, then cover and simmer gently for 40 minutes. Season with salt and freshly ground black pepper. Cover again and continue to simmer gently until the flageolets are cooked and soft, skimming occasionally. This will probably take another 30 minutes at least; the exact timing will depend on the freshness and quality of the flageolets.

When the flageolets are cooked, drain them well. Swirl in the butter and snip in the parsley before serving.

Haricots en Boîte Améliorés
Improved Canned Haricot Beans

I WAS BROUGHT up not to have any qualms about using canned haricot and flageolet beans. Look for *flageolets extra fins* in particular. They are worth stocking up on and excellent with lamb, sausages or bacon.

450-g can of flageolets or haricot beans	Serves 4	1 large ripe tomato
1 clove of garlic		1 tablespoon olive oil
1 large white Spanish onion or several button onions		15 g butter
		sea salt
		freshly ground black pepper

DRAIN AND COPIOUSLY RINSE THE canned beans. Finely chop the garlic and the large onion, if using. If using button onions, blanch them for several minutes in boiling water; drain well. Blanch the tomato, then peel, seed and chop it.

Heat the olive oil in a sauté pan. Add the garlic, prepared onion or button onions and tomato. Sauté gently for a few minutes, until softened. Add the drained beans and 6 tablespoons of water. Heat through over a low heat, stirring a few times. Drain once the beans are hot. Tip into a serving dish, swirl in the butter and season to taste. Serve hot.

Champignons Farcis
Stuffed Mushrooms

A GUTSY AND BUTTERY dish worth serving as a separate course.

4 very large or 8 medium-size undamaged, flat mushrooms	Serves 4	several sprigs each of parsley and chives
olive oil and butter for greasing	2 canned anchovy fillets or 2 teaspoons anchovy paste	3 tablespoons breadcrumbs made from day-old bread
FOR THE STUFFING	2 or 3 cloves of garlic	sea salt
120 g butter		freshly ground black pepper

HEAT THE OVEN TO 190°C/GAS 5. WIPE the mushrooms and break or cut off the stems. Trim off the gritty bottom ends, then finely chop the rest of the stems; reserve. Use either individual round gratin dishes or a large dish. Grease well first with oil, then with butter.

Prepare the stuffing: whizz together the butter, chopped mushroom stems, anchovy fillets (drained of their oil) or anchovy paste, garlic, parsley, chives and breadcrumbs in a food processor. Using a spatula, spread the stuffing over the mushroom caps. Season lightly with salt and more generously with freshly ground black pepper. Arrange the mushrooms in the gratin dishes or dish. Bake for about 30 minutes, until the mushrooms are soft and the stuffing golden. Serve hot.

CHAMPIGNONS À LA POÊLE
Pan-Fried Mushrooms

Oyster mushrooms are called *pleurotes* in French (from the Greek word for 'little ear'). Whether they look to you and me like bivalves or ears, both names are charmingly appropriate. On a recent visit to a mushroom farm near Vouvray in the Loire valley, I saw them growing commercially in a constantly lit cellar for the first time. Here they were, in fact, very mussel- rather than oyster-like, in clusters on a wall of well-insulated manure.

The owner of the place enjoyed hearing about their English name. *Très amusant, mais* ... Before I could add pedantically that their French name was very apt, too, she told me just why *pleurotes* are called *pleurotes*. These mushrooms, she explained, give of their best if you cook them briefly in a little hot fat, then let them weep (*pleurer*) a while before you finish the cooking. And that, Madame, is how they got their name.

Serves 6

225 g oyster mushrooms
1 tablespoon oil
60 g butter
sea salt
450 g brown cap mushrooms
2 or 3 cloves of garlic
several sprigs of parsley
freshly ground black pepper
1 lemon wedge, if liked
a few sprigs of chives, if liked

Heat the oil and a knob of butter in a large frying pan. Break the oyster mushrooms if they look unwieldy. Sauté the oyster mushrooms over a moderately high heat for a few minutes, stirring frequently. Season with a little salt. Remove the mushrooms from the pan with a draining spoon and spread them over a double layer of paper towels. Reduce the heat and add the rest of the butter to the pan.

Trim the brown caps and cut them in half, or quarters if they are on the large side. Crush the garlic. Put the mushrooms and garlic in the pan and stir to coat in the melted butter; season with a little salt. Turn up the heat just a notch and sauté the mushrooms for several minutes, until they are nearly cooked to your liking.

Stir in the reserved oyster mushrooms. Snip in the parsley and sauté for a couple of minutes; sprinkle with a little lemon juice and snip in some chives just before serving.

TOMATES FARCIES BIJOU
Herb-Stuffed Tomatoes

MY MOTHER'S WAY of stuffing tomatoes – perfect if you have access to a summer garden and also not bad with dried herbs. Particularly recommended with roast lamb and chicken dishes.

	Serves 4	
8 firm but ripe, medium-sized tomatoes		a few sprigs of as many of the following as you like: sweet savoury, thyme, oregano and marjoram
sea salt		
1 or 2 cloves of garlic		
3 tablespoons good olive oil		1 teaspoon sugar, if liked
2 tablespoons breadcrumbs made from day-old bread	several sprigs each of parsley, chervil, chives and tarragon	30 g butter
		freshly ground black pepper

SLICE OFF THE TOMATO TOPS. USING A small, sharp knife and a teaspoon, carefully remove the seeds and pulp. Sprinkle the tomatoes with a little salt. Place them upside down on paper towels and leave to drain for at least 20 minutes. Heat the oven to 180°C/Gas 4.

Very finely chop the garlic. Heat half the olive oil in a small saucepan and sauté the chopped garlic and breadcrumbs over a very moderate heat for a couple of minutes. Pour the sautéed garlic and breadcrumbs into a bowl. Snip in the fresh herbs and add a teaspoon of sugar, if liked. Stir until mixed.

Using a teaspoon, fill the tomatoes with the herb mixture. Put a knob of butter on top of each and season with freshly ground black pepper. Grease a gratin dish with the rest of the oil and put in the tomatoes. Cook in the bottom of the oven for 45 minutes to 1 hour. Reduce the heat a little if the tomatoes are collapsing. Serve warm.

POMMES DE TERRE À LA FORESTIÈRE
Sautéed Potatoes with Mushrooms and Bacon

THIS IS NOT so much a recipe as a way of combining two dishes to make a substantial main course.

CHOP 6 SLICES OF THICK-CUT UNSMOKED bacon. Turn to *pommes de terre sautées* on page 124. Add the chopped bacon to the rinsed and diced potatoes and follow Madame Boucher's recipe, trying not to rush the process. When the potatoes are half cooked, start preparing *champignons à la poêle*, using a sauté pan (see page 132). Combine the contents of the pans and serve with a large, sharply dressed green salad. Enough for 8.

Lentilles aux Lardons
Lentils with Bacon

I LOVE LENTILS. The lentils that come from Le Puy, in the heart of the volcanic Auvergne region of central France, are the very best and worth looking for. The bacon in the dish below is a well-tried combination, but I sometimes omit it if I am in a vegetarian mood or serving the lentils as a side dish. Try this with roast chicken and, dare I say it, creamed potatoes (see page 123).

For a lighter dish, omit the onion, tomato and bacon. Replace with a generous cup of chopped parsley, half at the beginning of cooking and the rest at the end. This version is best served *tiede*.

300 g *lentilles du Puy* or small
  dark blue-green lentils
1 onion
1 clove of garlic
1 large ripe tomato
60 g thick-cut rindless smoked
  back bacon

Serves 4

1 tablespoon olive oil
30 g butter
a few sprigs of parsley and
  thyme
1 bay leaf
sea salt
freshly ground black pepper

SOAK THE LENTILS WHILE YOU PREPARE the other ingredients. Finely chop the onion and garlic. Blanch, seed and chop the tomato. Cut the bacon in half; chop one half into small dice.

Drain and rinse the lentils. In a large, heavy-based saucepan, heat half the olive oil and a knob of butter. Add the chopped onion to the pan. Sauté over a moderate heat for a few minutes, then add the garlic and the lentils. Stir to mix with the onion and coat with the fat, then add the tomato and the unchopped half of bacon.

Add the herbs, including the bay leaf, then pour in plenty of water to completely cover the ingredients by at least 2.5 cm. Bring to

the boil fairly slowly, then season lightly with salt and freshly ground black pepper. Cover, reduce the heat and cook for 25 to 30 minutes, until the lentils are soft but not mushy. Lift the lid every now and then to check the cooking and add a ladleful of extra water if necessary.

When the lentils are nearly cooked, heat the rest of the oil in a small frying pan. Sauté the chopped bacon over a moderate heat until crisp and golden; drain on paper towels. Drain the lentils of any excess liquid. Discard the herbs and bay leaf. Slice the piece of bacon and return to the lentils. Swirl in the rest of the butter. Sprinkle in the sautéed bacon and serve immediately.

Endives au Four
Baked Chicory

CHICORY IS A BIT of an acquired taste. As children we certainly didn't rate it much. More often than not, we used to eat chicory plainly steamed, which we didn't at all like. Sometimes pan-fried with butter, which was an improvement and, less frequently, baked as below. This was a real treat, especially when the chicory was wrapped in thin slices of ham before being returned to the oven for the final *gratin* stage. I now prefer this dish without ham, but then I like the slightly bitter flavour of chicory a great deal more than I used to.

Serves 4

60 g butter
800 g chicory
2 teaspoons sugar
sea salt
freshly ground black pepper
1 lemon wedge
3 tablespoons *crème fraîche* or
    double cream
30 g Gruyère cheese

HEAT THE OVEN TO 180°C/GAS 4. THEN soften half the butter. Trim and rinse the chicory; discard any bruised outer leaves. Spread the softened butter over a gratin dish just large enough to take the chicory in a single layer.

Arrange the chicory in the dish. Sprinkle with sugar, then season lightly with salt and freshly ground black pepper. Squeeze the wedge of lemon over the chicory. Dot with the rest of the butter and cover with foil. Bake in the oven for about 30 minutes.

Grate the Gruyère into a bowl and combine with the *crème fraîche*. Season with a little black pepper. Take the dish out of the oven. Turn up the heat to 200°C/Gas 6. Remove the foil, then spread the cream and cheese mixture over the chicory. Return the dish to the oven and bake for 10 to 15 minutes, until golden and sizzling. Serve hot.

DESSERTS
Desserts

WHEN I WAS A CHILD, desserts were a treat and I still think of them as such – something sweet and quite special to delight in when the occasion warrants.

My mother did not have a sweet tooth and she was concerned about *la ligne*, not so much hers, which was most elegant, but that of her three daughters who were less streamlined. The result was that we seldom ate desserts at home, twice a week at the most. The national average is probably closer to once a day.

Instead we had cheese followed by fruit. We loved the former and dutifully munched the latter – to this day I much prefer eating fruit between meals, without knife and fork. Reading recently that it is healthier to ingest fruit on its own during a meal made me feel righteous and vindicated.

Looking back on this absence of daily dessert, I am grateful for two reasons. The first is that I soon became a cheese lover, with a wealth of pleasures and interesting finds in store, not only in France, but now magnificently in Britain. The second reason is that I was spared a lot of bad and filling sweet stodge. To my mind a boring dessert simply is not worth eating.

The French think of *pâtisserie* as an art. Like other families we relied on the best local master baker and bought in elaborate cakes and ice creams. What we did at home was the object of intense discussions and comparison – after all this was no routine matter. Why did this *tarte Tatin* go wrong? Was not the *île flottante* particularly light? Perhaps there was too much orange flavouring in the chocolate cake . . . All the recipes in the shortish repertoire that follows repeatedly passed the family test.

POMMES MERINGUÉES
Meringue Apples

A GREAT HOMELY pudding that is easy to make and likely to delight the whole family, from the very young to the very old via most reasonably self-indulging adults. I am reminded of a celebrated *Tintin* slogan that really sums up the range of family enjoyment – *pour tous les jeunnes de 7 à 77 ans*, for all the young between the ages of 7 and 77. Does conscious enjoyment start at 7 and end at 77, I sometimes wonder? I know I liked Mado's meringue apples years before I reached the Age of Reason and my grandfather, who is turning 97 at the time I am writing, still much favours them.

I like to use Cox's apples to make this pudding – the great sharp English Bramleys tend to collapse a little too readily.

This is not a difficult dessert to make, but do not rush it and allow plenty of cooling time between the various steps, to help the moisture escape and the meringue to crisp.

The *crème pâtissière* – made with more milk than usual – is light and fairly thin.

800 g Cox's apples
butter for greasing
110 g caster sugar
3 large egg whites

Serves 6 to 8

FOR THE *CRÈME PÂTISSIÈRE*
800 ml milk
1 vanilla pod, split, or a few
drops of vanilla essence

3 large egg yolks
75 g caster sugar
2 heaped tablespoons flour

MAKE THE *CRÈME PÂTISSIÈRE*. BRING THE milk to the boil n a saucepan with the split vanilla pod or a few drops of vanilla essence. Turn off the heat and, if using a vanilla pod, allow the milk to steep for 10 minutes.

Meanwhile, whisk together in a large bowl the egg yolks and sugar until the mixture is smooth and pale. Sift the flour into the egg and sugar mixture, then whisk again until well combined. Return the milk to the boil if necessary. Pour the boiling milk into the mixture and whisk until smooth and well blended.

Pour the mixture back into the pan and bring to the boil, stirring very frequently. Keep it bubbling for at least 5 minutes, still stirring frequently, to give the flour plenty of time to cook. Leave the *crème pâtissière* to cool, giving it the occasional stir to stop a skin from forming. Heat the oven to 180°C/Gas 4. Peel, quarter, core and thickly slice the apples.

Grease a large baking dish. Arrange the apple slices in the dish as evenly as possible. Sprinkle them with 1 tablespoon or so of sugar. Put the dish in the oven and cook the apples for 15 to 20 minutes – they should be just tender but not disintegrating. Remove the dish from the oven and leave the apples to cool a little. Turn the oven down to 170°C/Gas 3. Pour or spoon the *crème pâtissière* over the cooled apples.

Whisk the egg whites until very firm, then gradually add the sugar, a little at a time, still whisking. Spoon carefully or pipe the beaten egg whites over the *crème pâtissière*. If necessary, use a fork or the handle of a spoon to make an attractive pattern. Leave a few very tiny gaps to allow any steam to escape from the *crème pâtissière* – this will help the meringue to crisp. Return the dish to the oven and bake for at least 20 minutes, or until the meringue is golden and crisp. Serve hot or warm.

Pêches au Vin
Peaches in White Wine

Pêches au vin were a summer treat and a Fourchettes institution. In their crudest form, they were an unceremonious do-it-yourself-at-the-table concoction. While carrying on with the general conversation, you took an unpeeled peach, freshly plucked from the garden, chopped it up and tipped it into your wineglass. You then added a little wine – white, rosé or red, depending on what you were drinking at the time – and maybe a sprinkling of sugar. As children we made a happy sugary mush in our water glasses. I can recommend the method outlined above, especially if you have a glut of bruised peaches. Steep them in lightly sugared wine and chill for an hour or so for a lovely casual dessert.
The recipe below is more formal and definitely more refined. You may like to compromise between the two.

4 white peaches
300 ml white wine
1 vanilla pod
45 g sugar
2 tablespoons blackberry
  liqueur, *cassis* or red fruit
  liqueur

Serves 4

3 tablespoons redcurrant jelly
8 almonds, shelled and
  blanched
45 g shelled pistachios
a few mint leaves

PÊCHES BLANCHES
AU SIROP

Peel the peaches. Plunge them in a saucepan of boiling water and keep it bubbling for a couple of minutes. Lift the peaches out of the water with a draining spoon – the peel should slip off easily. If not, boil a minute more.

Prepare the syrup. In a saucepan large enough to take the peaches in a single layer, combine the wine with the same quantity of water. Slit the vanilla pod in half and add to the liquid. Stir in the sugar and bring to the boil, then reduce the heat and simmer until you have peeled the peaches.

Then add the peeled peaches to the simmering liquid and gently poach for 5 minutes, turning them over carefully halfway through. Remove the peaches from the poaching liquid with a draining spoon and leave them to cool a little.

Turn up the heat and boil the liquid until reduced by half. Stir in the blackberry or other liqueur and the redcurrant jelly. Carefully cut each peach in half. Remove the stones and place almonds in the cavities. Pour or spoon the syrup over the peaches.

Finely chop the shelled pistachios or, if you prefer, pound them using a mortar and pestle. Sprinkle the pistachios over the peaches and leave to macerate until cold, then chill until the dessert is needed. Arrange a mint leaf or two on top of each halved peach before serving.

Poires au Vin Rouge
Pears in Red Wine

A LATE SUMMER and autumn dessert popular all over France. The prunes are a traditional Loire ingredient, sadly fast disappearing and much harder to find locally these days. For the addition of *crème de cassis* and the *broiche* suggestion I am indebted to a professional chef, my friend Ghislaine Salé of the *Auberge de la Brenne* in Neuillé Le Lierre, between Amboise and Châteaurenault. My original family recipe was somewhat more basic. Use handsome, firm pears in peak condition for this recipe.

4 ripe-but-firm Williams pears	Serves 4	8 stoned prunes
600 ml red wine		2 tablespoons *crème de cassis*
1 to 2 tablespoons sugar		little hot *brioches*, to serve, if
1 tablespoon grated nutmeg		liked

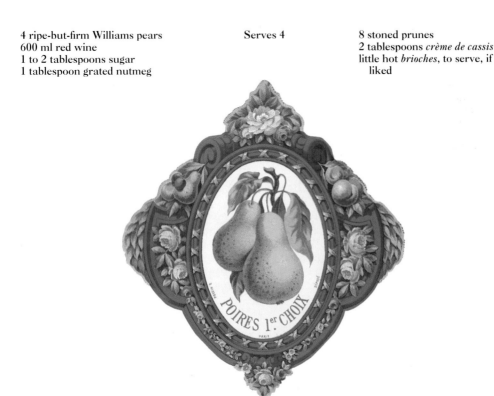

PEEL THE PEARS, KEEPING THEM WHOLE. In a heavy-based saucepan large enough to hold the pears comfortably in a single layer, combine the wine, sugar and nutmeg. Place the pears side by side in the liquid. Bring to a simmer. Add the prunes and simmer gently for about 15 minutes, until the pears are just cooked and tender.

Carefully turn the pears over once during cooking and baste occasionally with the simmering wine.

Using a draining spoon, remove the pears and prunes from the liquid. Leave to cool on a serving dish or in individual coupes; the pears look best upright.

Turn up the heat, add the *crème de cassis* to the wine and boil until the liquid becomes a little syrupy and is reduced by half. Spoon or pour the syrup over the pears and prunes and serve *tiède* or chilled. If you are serving the pears *tièdes*, hot *brioches* make a splendid accompaniment.

COMPOTE D'ABRICOTS ET DE FRAISES
Apricot and Strawberry Compote

THE TRICK WITH COMPOTES is not to allow the fruit to collapse into a purée. I like the combination below very much. It tastes even better if the raw strawberries you add at the end are *fraises des bois*, wild strawberries.

150 g sugar
1 vanilla pod
750 g ripe firm apricots

Serves 6

350 g ripe strawberries
½ lemon

IN A SAUCEPAN, COMBINE 300 ML WATER with the sugar. Split the vanilla pod and add to the liquid. Bring to the boil, then simmer while you halve and stone the apricots. Add the halved apricots to the simmering liquid and continue to simmer for 8 to 10 minutes. Meanwhile, rinse the strawberries under cold running water, then hull them.

Remove the apricots from the pan with a draining spoon and place in a bowl. Turn up the heat and bring the syrup to the boil.

Reduce it a little, then add half the strawberries. Turn down the heat and cook very gently for a few minutes. Remove the vanilla pod (dry and keep to use again), then add the poached strawberries and the syrup to the apricots. Stir, very gently, to mix.

Squeeze the lemon and, if they are very large, halve the rest of the strawberries. Add to the compote, sprinkle with the lemon juice and very gently stir the mixture. Refrigerate for at least 1 hour. Serve chilled.

CRÈME ANGLAISE
Custard

A GREAT ALL-ROUNDER that can be flavoured with a dash of strong black coffee, grated orange or lemon zest, liqueur, or rum. *Crème anglaise* is very flexible; the quantities below are average. For a thicker, sweeter cream to serve, for example, with a fruit purée or compote, use less milk (450 ml) and more sugar (120 g).

2 vanilla pods or a few drops of
   vanilla essence
600 ml milk

Serves 4

3 large or 4 medium egg yolks
90 g caster sugar

IF YOU ARE USING VANILLA PODS, SPLIT them in half lengthways. Bring the milk to the boil with the vanilla flavouring. Turn off the heat and leave to cool. Meanwhile, in a separate saucepan, whisk together the egg yolks and sugar until smooth and pale.

Remove the vanilla pods, if using. Over a very low heat, pour the warm milk, a little at a time, into the egg yolk and sugar

mixture, stirring well. Bring the mixture almost, but not quite, to boiling point very slowly, stirring constantly with a large wooden spoon. Do not let it boil and take it off the heat occasionally while it is cooking.

Once the cream is cooked and thickened so it coats the back of the wooden spoon, strain it through a fine strainer. If you are serving it cold, stir occasionally as it cools.

ŒUFS À LA NEIGE

Eggs in the Snow

THIS IS A FAVOURITE PARTY DISH – light as a feather, festive looking and, last but not least, economical. Another advantage of *oeufs à la neige* is that they can be prepared a day or two ahead, and taste all the better for it.

900 ml milk
300 g caster sugar
2 vanilla pods
5 large eggs
6 sugared almonds

Serves 4 to 6

FOR THE CARAMEL
90 g caster sugar

BRING THE MILK TO THE BOIL IN A LARGE saucepan with half the sugar and the split vanilla pods. Keep an eye on the milk while it is coming to the boil. Separate the eggs; reserve the yolks. Whisk the whites until they begin to stiffen, then sprinkle in 2 tablespoons of sugar and whisk the mixture until very firm.

Lower the heat. Remove the vanilla pods from the milk, then scoop up 4 big spoonfuls of whisked egg white and poach them very gently in the simmering milk, for just over 1 minute on each side, flipping them over carefully. Remove the egg 'meringues' from the milk, drain well and reserve on a clean cloth. Repeat the process until you have used up all the whisked egg white, making sure that the milk never gets back up to boiling point.

Strain the milk. In a saucepan, beat the reserved egg yolks with the rest of the sugar until smooth and much paler in colour. Turn down the heat to very low. Pour the hot milk a little at a time into the egg-yolk mixture, stirring constantly with a wooden spoon, and cook very slowly until the cream begins to thicken. Never allow the mixture to boil. Take the pan off the heat occasionally and continue stirring until the cream is just thick enough to coat the back of the wooden spoon. Remove from the heat and leave the cream to cool completely, stirring it occasionally.

Pour the cooled cream into a large glass bowl and carefully arrange the cooked egg whites on top – they will float.

Prepare the caramel. In a medium-size saucepan, combine the sugar with 90 ml water, stirring until dissolved, then bring to the boil and continue boiling without stirring until you have a thick, rich brown syrup. Immediately trickle this sticky caramel syrup over the egg whites.

Roughly crush the sugared almonds – I use a mortar and pestle or the small bowl of my food processor – and sprinkle them over the dish. Refrigerate overnight and serve very cold.

Ile Flottante
Floating Island

Another fluffy and hard-to-resist egg dessert that can be prepared well in advance. I believe that *ile flottante* once described as a layered cake of *brioche* or sponge, apricot marmalade, almonds and dried raisins set on a custard or red fruit purée, but I have never personally encountered the old-style pudding.

	Serves 4 to 6	
3 large or 4 medium egg whites		To serve
120 g caster sugar		*crème anglaise* (see page 140) or
9 sugared almonds or 2 small	For the caramel	red fruit purée (see opposite)
dry macaroons	75 g caster sugar, or light	
	brown sugar	

Make the caramel. In a small saucepan, combine the sugar with 5 to 6 tablespoons of water. Stir until dissolved over a gentle heat, then turn up the heat and boil without stirring until the syrup turns golden brown. Pour at once into a *moule à manqué*, ring mould or charlotte mould and swirl to coat all over.

Coarsely crush the sugared almonds or macaroons using a mortar and pestle. Heat the oven to 170°C/Gas 3. Whisk the egg whites until firm, then gradually mix in the sugar and crushed sugared almonds or macaroons. Continue whisking until the meringue mixture is stiff.

Bring a full kettle of water to the boil. Line the bottom of a large roasting tin with several layers of newspaper. Pour the meringue mixture into the prepared mould. Put the mould in the centre of the lined roasting tin. Pour in boiling water to come halfway up the sides of the mould. Cook the meringue in this *bain-marie* for about 40 minutes, keeping an eye on the level of the water; pour in extra boiling water if necessary.

Leave the floating island to cool completely before unmoulding it on to a serving dish.

Serve chilled, over *crème anglaise* or red fruit purée. If using red fruit purée, stir into it the juice of a lemon and then sweeten to taste with icing sugar rather than using caster sugar.

Glace Double à la Vanille et aux Fruits Rouges

Vanilla and Red Fruit Ice Cream

This is a good ice cream for the berry season. Use the egg whites to make meringues.

600-g mixture of some, or all,
of the following:
strawberries, raspberries,
blackberries, redcurrants
150 g caster sugar
600 ml double cream
strawberries and raspberries,
to serve, if liked

Serves 8 to 10

FOR THE *CRÈME ANGLAISE*
350 ml full-fat milk
3 vanilla pods or several drops
of vanilla essence
4 medium egg yolks
120 g caster sugar

MAKE A THICK *CRÈME ANGLAISE* (SEE PAGE 140), strain it through a fine strainer or *chinois* and whisk it frequently while it gets cold. Rinse and clean the fruit. Purée in the food processor, then press the purée through a strainer into a bowl. Stir the sugar into the fruit purée until absorbed.

Whip the thick cream until firm. Reserve about one-third of the whipped cream and carefully fold the rest into the fruit purée. Pour or spoon the fruit and cream mixture into a tray and freeze.

Fold the reserved whipped cream into the cold custard. Flavour with a little extra vanilla essence if you like. Pour the mixture into a second tray of the same size as the first tray and freeze. After 30 to 40 minutes, remove both iced preparations from the freezer and stir to prevent ice crystals from forming. Repeat the process twice, then leave until frozen – the vanilla ice cream is less likely to crystallise than the other.

Remove the trays from the freezer about 10 minutes before serving and serve the vanilla ice cream on top of the red fruit ice cream in a serving dish. If you like, surround the ice-cream sandwich with extra strawberries and raspberries.

CERISES LÉGISLATIVES
Cherry Ring

A JOLLY WAY TO enhance plain vanilla ice cream, bearing a jokey title which, for the French, has republican or even revolutionary overtones.

450 g sweet ripe cherries
40 g unsalted butter
60 g caster sugar
the juice of 1 large orange

Serves 4 to 6

the juice of 1 large lemon
2 tablespoons kirsh
2 tablespoons *crème de cassis*
vanilla ice cream, to serve

RINSE THE CHERRIES AND REMOVE THE stems and remove the stems and stones. In a heavy-based saucepan, melt the butter over a low heat.

Add the stoned cherries, sugar and orange and lemon juices and simmer gently for 5 to 10 minutes, stirring delicately every now and then.

Drain the cherries over a bowl. Reserve the cherries and return the poaching juices to the pan. Bring to a simmer and reduce by about one-third. Add the kirsh and *crème de cassis*, then bring to the boil and bubble for 2 to 3 minutes.

Meanwhile, arrange the cherries around piled-up scoops of vanilla ice cream. If you are serving this dessert in individual cups, allow 3 scoops per person. Spoon the sauce over the ice cream and serve immediately.

GÂTEAU À L'ORANGE
Orange Cake

ANOTHER RECIPE FROM MY aunt Yonnée, which brings back hazy memories of my grandmother, mother and aunts rather reluctantly hosting a ladies' tea. For that old-fashioned institution, *le goûter de dames*, the finest china came out and best behaviour was *de rigueur*. We all watched from a safe distance.

125 g caster sugar
90 g soft unsalted butter, plus
    extra for greasing
2 large eggs

Serves 6

125 g self-raising flour
1 scant teaspoon baking
    powder
1 large juicy orange
1 tablespoon Cointreau

FOR THE GLAZING
75 ml orange juice
1 tablespoon Cointreau
110 to 125 g icing sugar

HEAT THE OVEN TO 180°C/GAS 4. BEAT together the sugar and butter until creamy. Beat in the eggs. Sift the flour and baking powder over the mixture and fold in lightly.

Grate the zest of the orange and squeeze out the juice. Stir zest, juice and Cointreau into the batter. Then grease a 1.2-litre loaf tin and spoon in the batter. Knock the tin against the work surface to settle the contents. Bake for about 50 minutes, until the cake is firm but bouncy to the touch and the blade of a knife inserted into it comes out clean. Leave it to cool for 10 to 15 minutes, then unmould on to a dish.

Meanwhile, prepare the glazing. In a small saucepan, gently warm the orange juice and Cointreau. Stir in the icing sugar.

Using a pastry brush, paint the glaze over the cake – some of the glaze will seep in, the rest will form a light crust. Serve cold.

Gâteau Glacé au Moka
Iced Mocha Gâteau

Hard to resist. I tend to prefer this grown-up dessert without the optional extras, but candied angelica and cherries make fine additions.

200 g bitter chocolate
2 tablespoons good-quality
   instant coffee granules
200 g caster sugar
200 g unsalted butter, plus
   extra for greasing
5 medium eggs
sea salt

Serves 6 to 8

90 ml brandy
45 ml kirsch
27 to 30 *biscuits à la cuiller* or
   36 ladyfingers

To serve (optional)
candied mixed fruit
candied cherries

Break the chocolate into small pieces and place in a heavy-based saucepan with 120 ml boiling water. Leave to stand for 3 minutes, then pour out the water and stir the chocolate over a very low heat until creamy.

Stir in the coffee granules, then set aside the pan over a bowl of boiling water, giving this cream an occasional stir.

Meanwhile, whisk together the sugar and butter until pale golden and foamy.

Separate the eggs, one at a time, collecting the whites in a large bowl and whisking each yolk into the sugar and butter. Whisk the mixture well after adding each yolk.

When all the yolks have been incorporated, whisk in the chocolate and coffee cream, a little at a time. If it feels too thick and solid, beat in a tablespoon or two of hot water before adding to the butter, sugar and yolk mixture.

Add a pinch of salt to the egg whites and whisk until stiff. Now fold the whisked egg whites into the chocolate mixture, using a large metal spoon or balloon whisk, which-ever you are most comfortable with. Start by folding in a couple of spoonfuls, then tip in the rest. The important thing is to work lightly and with upward movements to get air into the mixture. Stop working as soon as the egg whites are absorbed.

Generously butter a large 2.5-litre loaf tin. Combine the brandy and kirsch with 3 tablespoons water in a soup plate. Quickly dip each biscuit into this mixture and line the bottom of the loaf tin with a layer of biscuits; continue with a second layer of biscuits.

Spoon in the chocolate and coffee mousse. Knock the tin once or twice against the work surface to settle the contents. Then cover the top with 2 layers of biscuits soaked in the brandy mixture.

Freeze overnight or for several hours, making sure the freezer is not turned to the highest/coldest setting.

Remove the iced gâteau from the freezer a few minutes before serving. Turn out on to a long platter. If you like, arrange pieces of candied fruit around the gateau.

Tarte au Citron
Lemon Tart

This is my version of my sister Françoise's recipe, which she jotted down a long time ago at our cousin Florence's . . . It is sharp, zesty and a most pleasing way to round off a meal.

Serves 6

For the pastry base
150 g unsalted butter, plus extra for greasing
1 large egg
75 g caster sugar
a small pinch of salt

250 g flour, plus extra for flouring

For the filling
120 g unsalted butter

200 g caster sugar
1 unwaxed orange
3 unwaxed juicy lemons
3 large or 5 medium eggs

Leave the butter in a warm place until softened. Prepare the pastry base. In a bowl, whisk the egg with the sugar and a small pinch of salt until the mixture is light and foamy. Sift the flour into a second bowl, then tip it all at once into the egg and sugar mixture. Work the mixture lightly with your fingertips until it begins to feel like coarse sand. Cut the softened butter into small pieces and work into the mixture until the pastry is smooth. Roll the pastry into a ball and refrigerate for at least 1 hour.

Heat the oven to 180°C/Gas 4. Dust a rolling pin with flour and generously butter a tart tin. Roll out the pastry and line the prepared tin – I invariably end up using my hands to flatten the pastry and fit it into the tin, as it is very 'short', breaking easily.

Now make the filling. Combine the softened butter with the sugar, beating vigorously until the mixture is smooth.

Finely grate the orange and 1 or 2 lemons – the more zest you use, the sharper and more lemony the filling. Squeeze all the lemons. Whisk the eggs a little longer than you would for an omelette. Stir the grated zests and the lemon juice into the butter and sugar mixture. Whisk in the beaten eggs.

Pour the filling into the prepared pastry case and bake for 35 to 40 minutes, until the filling is set and the base cooked. Cool before you remove the tart from the tin.

Tatin Express
Quick Upside-Down Apple Tart

NOT THE REAL THING, but very good indeed if you are pushed for time. The shortcut idea came from my cousin Isabelle, who is a great believer in never spending more than a few minutes at a time in her kitchen.

Serves 6

750 g crisp eating apples
60 g soft unsalted butter, plus
   extra to finish
90 g caster sugar, plus extra to
   finish

225 g ready-made shortcrust
   pastry, rolled out slightly
   larger than the pan

HEAT THE OVEN AND A LARGE BAKING tray to 200°C/Gas 6. Very generously butter the base and sides of a loose-bottomed tart tin. Sprinkle liberally with sugar. Quarter and core the apples, then arrange them evenly and tightly in the prepared tin. Sprinkle the apples with the rest of the sugar and dot with the rest of the butter. Place the sheet of prepared pastry over the apples. Trim and fit it in all around between the apples and the sides of the tin.

Place the tin on the hot baking tray and bake for 20 to 25 minutes, until the pastry is cooked and golden. Check after 10 or 15 minutes and lower the heat if the pastry is browning too quickly.

Remove the tin from the oven and let it cool for a good 15 minutes. When it is cool enough to handle comfortably, cover the tin with a serving dish, then carefully turn both tin and dish upside down. Now remove the ring and bottom, easing them off the tart with a knife if necessary. Dot the tart with a little extra butter and sprinkle it with a little more sugar. Pop it under a hot grill until the butter and sugar bubble. Serve warm.

TARTE TATIN
Caramelised Upside-Down Apple Tart

A WONDERFUL, BUT tricky, dish, with an infuriating tendency either to burn or not to caramelise enough. You can make a *Tatin* in a deep flameproof flan tin, but it helps enormously if you use the proper French pan, a *moule à manqué*, which is round and about 5 cm deep. I have just invested in a heavy-based stainless-steel mould that conveniently comes with its own serving dish. A good kitchen equipment store should be able to supply you with a *moule à manqué*.

I would love to take part in a *Tatin* workshop – every cook who 'does' this dessert seems to have a different recipe. The method below is the one I am happiest with at the moment. I add 'at the moment' because it is likely to evolve: the sprinkling of sugar over the pastry is something I have only just started doing. To give credit where it is due, let me explain that it is a little *truc* my sister Anne-Sophie kindly let me in to the last time I congratulated her on the crispness of her *Tatin* pastry.

Serves 6 to 8

1.2 kg crisp eating apples, such as Cox's	FOR THE PASTRY	2 tablespoons *crème fraîche* or sour cream
120 g soft unsalted butter	225 g flour	
150 g caster sugar	1 tablespoon caster sugar, plus extra to sprinkle	TO SERVE (OPTIONAL)
	a small pinch of salt	Calvados
	150 g soft unsalted butter	*crème fraîche* or sour cream

PREPARE THE PASTRY. SIFT THE FLOUR into a bowl, add the sugar and salt and stir to combine. Cut the butter into small pieces, then work it into the flour with your fingertips. Once the butter has been absorbed, work in the *crème fraîche*. Roll into a ball, wrap in plastic wrap and chill for at least half an hour.

Melt half the butter in the tin. Remove from the heat. Sprinkle half the sugar over the melted butter and swirl to mix; make sure that the edge of the tin is well coated with butter and sugar.

Peel and core the apples. Cut them in half, which is traditional, or into chunky quarters, which I prefer. Arrange the apples over the butter and sugar, packing them in tightly. Sprinkle them with the rest of the sugar and dot with the rest of the butter.

Place on top of the stove over a moderately high heat for 10 to 15 minutes, until the butter and sugar look golden and lightly caramelised; keep a sharp eye on it to make sure the mixture does not turn too brown. Remove the pan from the heat and leave until just cool enough to handle. Heat the oven to 220°C/Gas 7.

Lightly dust a rolling pin with flour and roll out the pastry, not too thinly. Make sure that your circle of pastry is 5 cm larger than the tin. You may need to use your hands as well – this pastry tends to crumble. Place the rolled out pastry over the apples. Using your fingers, tuck it in well between the apples and the edge of the tin. Sprinkle a little sugar over the surface to make it more crunchy and prick in several places with a fork. Bake in the oven for about 30 minutes, until the pastry is golden.

Remove from the oven and leave to cool for a few minutes. Cover with a serving dish slightly larger than the pan you have used. *Tarte Tatin* is best served barely warm. Turn over and unmould on to the dish just before serving, knocking the serving dish against the work surface and tapping the tin sharply.

Rearrange the apples a little if necessary. Serve the *tarte* on its own, or sprinkled with Calvados and/or accompanied by a small bowl of *crème fraîche*, as you wish.

Petits Soufflés Fondants au Chocolat au Coulis de Framboises

Soft-Centred Chocolate Soufflés with Raspberry Sauce

WHEN IN DOUBT, I serve a hot chocolate dessert. Over the years I have tried a number of individual chocolate soufflés and chef-style fondants. This is the most fun to prepare and delicious to eat. Very conveniently, you can freeze the mixture in the ramekins, then bake from frozen for 20 minutes. Don't leave in the oven longer than instructed – the centre has to be runny. You can't go wrong, but I have to warn you that the texture is delightfully unpredictable. One of my 'students' called me the day after a demonstration to breezily ask if it was a safe dish to do. She was having 12 people to dinner. There was no time for a practice run. If you feel timid, don't turn the soufflés out the first time you try them. But resist the temptation to overcook: better a very runny fondant in a ramekin than a harder cake on a plate.

75 g soft unsalted butter, plus extra for greasing
30 g unsweetened cocoa powder, plus extra for dusting
175 g top-quality bitter chocolate

Serves 6

20 g self-raising flour
1½ tablespoons B&B (Benedictine and brandy), or 2 teaspoons each brandy and Cointreau
3 fresh eggs
175 g caster sugar

RASPBERRY COULIS FOR SERVING
400 g raspberries, fresh or frozen and defrosted
icing sugar to taste
1 tablespoon lemon juice

GREASE 6 INDIVIDUAL 10-CM RAMEKINS. Dust with cocoa powder and chill for at least 1 hour.

Make the raspberry coulis. Blast the raspberries in a blender or food processor until puréed. Push through a strainer, then rinse out the bowl of the blender or processor with 6 tablespoons of water. Add to the strainer and push through. Sweeten to taste with icing sugar, stir and add the lemon juice. Chill until needed.

Heat the oven to 190°C/Gas 5. Place a bowl over a saucepan of simmering water, making sure there is space between the bottom of the bowl and the water. Break the chocolate into small pieces. Place the chocolate in the bowl with the butter and leave to melt.

Separate the eggs. Put the whites into a large bowl, preferably copper or metal. In a second smaller bowl, lightly beat the yolks, as for an omelette.

Tip the sugar into a small saucepan, add 5 tablespoons water. Place over a moderate heat and leave to bubble gently until you have a pale golden syrup.

Meanwhile, whisk the egg whites until they stiffen into a meringue. Still whisking, trickle the syrup into the meringue. Whisk until well blended in; set aside.

Mix the flour and cocoa powder. Take the melted chocolate off the heat and sift in the flour and cocoa mixture. Leave to cool a little, whisk in the egg yolks, whisking until smooth. Gently fold the chocolate mixture into the meringue. Then spoon the mixture into the prepared ramekins and tap them against the work surface to make sure there are not any air bubbles. Bake for 15 minutes (20 if frozen) and no longer.

Invert the contents of the ramekins on to plates before serving. Add a trickle of the raspberry coulis and finally dust with extra cocoa powder.

Mousse au Chocolat
Chocolate Mousse

TOO MANY NASTY concoctions go under the name of chocolate mousse – mean little messes of chocolatey *ersatz* and gluey gelatine, in small plastic tubs or large institutional bowls. To my mind chocolate mousse belongs in the home. All you need is good-quality dark chocolate, eggs, unsalted butter, a little sugar and maybe a dash of spirits. You can then concoct a generous dessert that few will resist. A proper chocolate mousse should be deep brown, glossy and close textured. Not a particle of gelatine in sight, just lashings of chocolate held together smoothly by the eggs and butter.

I like to flavour the chocolate with Cointreau, but whisky, rum or brandy also work well.

150 g best dark chocolate 60 g soft unsalted butter 2 eggs, at room temperature	Serves 5 or 6	3 egg whites, at room temperature 1 or 2 tablespoons caster sugar a dash of Cointreau (optional)

BREAK THE CHOCOLATE INTO SMALL pieces. Grease a saucepan with a little of the butter, then melt the chocolate completely over a very low heat, stirring occasionally with a wooden spoon; keep the heat very low throughout. As soon as the chocolate melts, remove the pan from the heat and stir in the rest of the butter until it completely melts.

Carefully break the eggs, putting the whites into a large bowl and making sure they are entirely free of yolk. Gently stir the yolks into the chocolate mixture until they are thoroughly absorbed, then leave to cool. When the mixture is almost at room temperature, whisk the egg whites until thick and foamy. Add the sugar and whisk until stiff and slightly glossy peaks form.

Using a large metal spoon or balloon whisk, fold a spoonful of whisked egg white into the chocolate mixture; mix it in well. Stir in a dash of Cointreau, if liked. Fold in the rest with a metal spoon or balloon whisk. The important thing is to work lightly with upward movements to get as much air as possible into the mixture. Stop working as soon as the egg whites are completely absorbed.

Pour the mousse into a serving dish, stemmed glasses or ramekins and refrigerate overnight, or for at least 3 hours.

Charlotte aux Amandes et aux Pistaches

Almond and Pistachio Charlotte

THE FACT THAT charlottes were probably a tribute to King George III's wife and could therefore be regarded as an English dessert is largely forgotten in France, where they are a popular family dessert. The word is used very loosely, but charlottes tend to be a mousse, *bavaroise* or bombe mixture encased in biscuits soaked in liqueur or coffee and chilled in a deep, round mould, wider at the top than at the bottom. The recipe below impressed many a dinner-party guest at my parents' table, served on a fine white china-stemmed dish with a pale green and gold rim. I used to think that the green of the dish matching the pistachios was the height of refinement. With the considerable amount of kirsch absorbed by the biscuits, this is no nursery dessert but, on charlotte nights, we always stayed awake until we could hear the guests and our parents safely ensconced back in the sitting room after dinner. The nutty, boozy, exciting leftovers were then ours to feast on like sleepy vultures. This winner of a dessert is very conveniently made the day before the party.

20 to 24 *biscuits à la cuiller*, or about 30 ladyfingers
kirsch
225 g caster sugar, plus a little extra to sweeten the water
1 large egg
250 g soft unsalted butter

Serves 6 to 8

250 g finely ground blanched almonds
90 g shelled pistachio nuts, grated
crème anglaise (see page 140), to serve

SOAK THE BISCUITS OR LADYFINGERS IN A mixture of kirsch and water sweetened with sugar. Line the bottom of a 1.1-litre charlotte mould with biscuits, trimming them to shape, flat sides facing up. Then line the side of the mould with overlapping biscuits or ladyfingers, flat sides facing in.

Cream together the sugar, egg and butter until totally combined and smooth, then work in the ground almonds and half the grated pistachios. Flavour the mixture with kirsch and spoon it into the lined charlotte mould. Cover with soaked biscuits or lady-fingers. Top with a plate. Place a weight on the plate and chill overnight in the refrigerator. Keep the remaining pistachios wrapped in plastic wrap in the refrigerator as well.

To serve, carefully unmould the charlotte on to a serving plate; do not worry if some of the biscuits get a little damaged in the process. Pour some cold *crème anglaise* over it, thus concealing minor disasters and spoon more *crème anglaise* around the bottom of the charlotte. Sprinkle with the rest of the pistachios.

Profiteroles au Chocolat
Chocolate Profiteroles

MADO'S PROFITEROLES WERE absolutely top of the family pops, requested with amazing regularity for birthdays and other high days. *Crème pâtissière* is the more traditional filling, but we all loved vanilla ice cream. When I make this dessert these days, I use good-quality store-bought ice cream rather than make my own. *Paresseuse* – you lazy girl, said Mado, the last time we discussed the dish on the phone.

FOR THE CHOUX
120 g unsalted butter
150 g flour
250 ml water
salt
3 large or 4 medium eggs
dash of milk for glazing

Serves 6

FOR THE FILLING
vanilla ice cream or thick
crème pâtissière, made as on
page 137, but using only
300 ml milk

FOR THE CHOCOLATE SAUCE
120 g dark bitter chocolate
2 tablespoons caster sugar
2 tablespoons double cream
30 g unsalted butter

CUT THE BUTTER INTO DICE. SIFT THE flour on a sheet of greaseproof paper. In a heavy-based saucepan, bring the water to the boil with the diced butter and a very small pinch of salt. As soon as the liquid begins to boil, remove the pan from the heat. Quickly – and all at once – add the flour and immediately start stirring it in with a spatula or wooden spoon. Return the saucepan to the heat and continue to stir briskly until the paste comes off the pan and looks smooth and a little shiny.

Remove from the heat and stir for 1 minute more. Add the eggs one at a time, mixing them in vigorously until the paste comes together again. Beat the last egg before you add it in, since you may need only a fraction of it; you should end up with a glossy, floppy paste, not a runny, liquid one. Continue beating for a couple of minutes to give the paste more body.

Heat the oven to 190°C/Gas 5. Grease a baking tray. Fit a pastry bag with a plain 0.5-cm tip and spoon the paste into the bag. Pipe the paste on to the baking tray, shaping it into balls, about the size of a small tomato. Keep them at least 4 cm apart. If you do not like using a pastry bag, use a tablespoon instead – the end result will just look a little rougher. Brush the paste lightly with any remaining egg yolk mixed with a dash of milk.

Bake for about 30 minutes, until well risen and brown. Leave to stand 5 minutes in the oven before taking out, to dry the puffs a little. Slit the warm puffs sideways, almost but not quite in half, but wait until they are cold before you fill them.

If you are using *crème pâtissière*, you can fill the choux well ahead of serving. Spoon in a little of the *crème pâtissière* and keep in a cool place.

Break the chocolate into small pieces. Place the pieces in a saucepan with 120 ml water and the sugar. Melt over a very low heat, stirring frequently with a wooden spoon. When the mixture is smooth, stir in the cream. Take the pan off the heat and swirl in the butter, stirring until it is melted, to give the sauce a nice gloss.

If you are intending to fill the choux puffs with vanilla ice cream, do so after taking the chocolate sauce off the heat. Quickly spoon in the ice cream.

Pile the filled choux on a dish – they look much more attractive this way than in individual coupes. Pour over some chocolate sauce and serve the rest in a sauceboat.

LE GÂTEAU AU CHOCOLAT
Chocolate Cake

My idea of what a homemade chocolate cake should be: dark, rich, solid, irresistible and definitely for feast days. Over the years I have played with other ideas, but I always loyally come back to this recipe. In my experience this cake disappears pretty quickly, but it will keep nicely moist for several days in the refrigerator, wrapped loosely in foil. It also travels well and will make you a popular weekend or party guest – but leave making the coating until you have arrived with your gift. The coating is over the top and optional – but highly recommended.

200 g good quality bitter chocolate
150 g caster sugar
175 g soft unsalted butter, plus extra for greasing
3 heaped tablespoons self-raising flour

Serves 8

5 medium eggs
a small pinch of salt
grated zest of 1 small orange, or a dash of Cointreau, to flavour, if liked

FOR THE COATING (OPTIONAL)
200 g good quality bitter chocolate
200 ml single cream
4 walnuts, if liked

BREAK THE CHOCOLATE INTO SMALL PIECES. In a large, heavy-based saucepan, melt the chocolate pieces with 2 tablespoons of water over an extremely low heat, stirring frequently with a wooden spoon. Stir in the sugar and take the pan off the heat while you cut the butter.

Return the pan to a very low heat and stir in the butter, a little at a time. Now sift in the flour, stir lightly to combine and cook for a couple of minutes, still over a low heat. Remove the pan from the heat and let the mixture cool a little.

Meanwhile, heat the oven to 170°C/Gas 3 and generously butter a 2.5-litre loaf or cake tin.

Separate the eggs: the whites can be collected together in a large bowl, but the yolks should be put on individual saucers – or an oyster plate with its 'scoops' is helpful here. Work the yolks into the chocolate mixture, one at a time, beating them in thoroughly. Add a pinch of salt to the egg whites and whisk until very firm and stiff.

Using a large metal spoon, fold the whisked egg whites into the chocolate mixture very thoroughly, but working lightly and with upward movements. If you like, flavour with the grated zest of a small orange or a dash of Cointreau. Tip the batter into the greased tin and knock the tin on the work surface a couple of times to make sure the batter is evenly settled.

Bake for about 45 minutes. Resist opening the oven door for the first 25 minutes, then check and turn the tin around if the cake is looking lopsided. Turn up the heat to the next setting for the last 5 minutes – insert a knife into the cake to check that it is baked: the blade should come out clean and dry. Leave to cool for 15 minutes, then carefully remove the cake from the tin and place it on a serving dish.

If you decide to coat the cake, wait until it is cold. Break the chocolate into small pieces and melt it with the cream in a saucepan over a very low heat, stirring frequently with a wooden spoon. Leave the mixture to cool a little, then pour it over the centre of the cake. Have a soft spatula at hand to smooth the coating evenly over the whole surface. Carefully shell the walnuts to keep the halves as whole as possible and arrange them over the cake, if desired.

Gâteau aux Noix
Walnut Cake

The fresher the walnuts, the better this cake will taste. It begs to be served with a cup of properly made coffee, but I once enjoyed it with a very vinous glass of mature Cahors.

250 g fresh walnuts
3 medium eggs
225 g caster sugar
60 g self-raising flour, plus
    extra for flouring

Serves 6

1 tablespoon rum
butter for greasing

For the coating
90 g dark bitter chocolate
3 tablespoons single cream
30 g unsalted butter

Heat the oven to 180°C/Gas 4. Finely chop or pound the walnuts, reserving 9 attractive pieces. Separate the eggs. In a bowl, whisk together the sugar and egg yolks until smooth and pale. Stir in the chopped walnuts, then sift in the flour and sprinkle in the rum. Whisk lightly to combine.

In a separate bowl, whisk the egg whites until stiff, then delicately fold them into the mixture, using a large metal spoon. Work them in lightly, with upward movements, until absorbed.

Butter and flour a *moule à manquè* or deep flan tin. Pour the mixture into the prepared tin, knock the tin once or twice against the work surface to settle the contents. Bake the cake for 40 minutes, until it is firm to the touch. Leave to cool for a few minutes, then turn out on to a rack and leave until cold.

To make the coating, break the chocolate into small pieces. In a saucepan, combine the chocolate with 3 tablespoons of water and the cream. Heat slowly over a very low heat, stirring constantly with a wooden spoon, until the mixture is smooth. Take the pan off the heat and stir in the butter. Pour the coating over the centre of the cake and spread with a soft spatula. Arrange the reserved walnut pieces at regular intervals around the cake and place one in the centre.

QUATRE-QUARTS
French Pound Cake

LITERALLY MEANING FOUR QUARTERS – equal weights of egg, butter, sugar and flour – the French pound cake is a great standby, often served as a family dessert with stewed fruit compote (see page 140), fruit salad, or, mid-afternoon, with a cup of tea (a more popular beverage in France than rumour would have it). Lemon, vanilla and orange are all traditional discreet flavourings. The ground almonds are a family addition.

2 large or 3 medium eggs
150 g caster sugar
finely grated zest of 1 lemon or
   orange, or a little vanilla
   essence

Serves 4 to 6

150 g soft unsalted butter
150 g self-raising flour, plus
   extra for dusting
2 heaped tablespoons finely
   ground blanched almonds

HEAT THE OVEN TO 180°C/GAS 4. BEAT together the eggs, sugar and flavouring until pale and a little frothy. Pour the butter in a loaf tin or deep round *moule à manqué* tin and heat it in the oven until almost melted. Swirl to coat the tin lightly with butter, then pour the melted butter into the egg mixture a little at a time, whisking until thoroughly blended. Sift the flour over the egg and sugar mixture, a little at a time, then fold it in gently with a large metal spoon. Now fold in the ground almonds.

Dust the tin with a little flour, pour in the batter and bake for 30 to 35 minutes. If the top browns too quickly, cover it with a piece of foil. To check that the cake is cooked, insert a skewer. When the cake is done you will find that the skewer comes out clean and dry.

Turn out the cake on to a rack as soon as it comes out of the oven and leave to get cold before serving.

The cake will keep well for a few days wrapped in foil and refrigerated.

Index

All recipe titles are listed in French and English. Ingredients are indexed in English only.

agneau en papillote, 110
ale: rabbit with ale and prunes, 102
almonds: almond and pistachio charlotte, 151
   sea bream with almond stuffing, 81
anchoïade, 35
anchovies: anchovy purée, 35
   hard-boiled eggs with anchovy mayonnaise, 36
   Provençal onion and anchovy tart, 54
   steaks with pepper and anchovy, 118
starters, 28-39
apples: caramelised upside-down apple tart, 148
   meringue apples, 137
   quick upside-down apple tart, 147
apricot and strawberry compote, 140
asparagus: asparagus and herb vichyssoise, 25
aubergines: aubergine gratin, 127
   ragout of Provençal vegetables, 121
avocado: chilled spinach and avocado soup, 26
   sweet red pepper and avocado salad, 31

bacon: lentils with bacon, 134
   sautéed potatoes with mushrooms and bacon, 133
basil: vegetable soup with basil, garlic and cheese, 18
beef: beef cooked in red Burgundy, 114
   boiled beef with vegetables, 116
   braised beef, 117
   French cottage pie, 119
   slow-cooked beef casserole, 115
   steaks with pepper and anchovy, 118
beurre manié, 12
blanquette de veau, 104
bœuf bourguignon, 114
bœuf en daube, 115
bœuf mode, 117
brandade de morue, 76
butter, 12

cabbage: shredded cabbage salad, 39
cakes: chocolate cake, 153
   French pound cake, 155
   walnut cake, 154
canard aux navets, 97
canard aux olives, 96
canard aux pêches, 96

caramel: caramelised apple tart, 148
   eggs in the snow, 141
   floating island, 142
carottes au cumin, 125
carottes râpées, 39
carrots: carrots cooked with cumin, 125
   grated carrot salad, 39
   leek, carrot and potato soup, 22
   sautéed carrot and courgette ribbons, 126
cassoulet maison, 108
céleri rémoulade, 33
celery root (celeriac) mayonnaise, 33
cerises législatives, 144
champignons à la poêle, 132
champignons en salade, 32
champignons farcis, 130
charlotte aux amandes et aux pistaches, 151
chaudfroid de poulet, 87
cheese: cheese choux ring, 51
   cheese soufflé, 47
   gratin of eggs and Gruyère, 42
   hot cheese *croustades*, 49
   onion soup with Roquefort, 21
   Roquefort cheese puff, 50
   toasted cheese and ham, 49
cherries: cherry ring, 144
chicken: chicken *chaudfroid*, 87
   chicken cooked in red wine, 90
   chicken cooked in a wine and cream sauce, 91
   chicken stock, 12
   chicken with a vinegar sauce, 89
   huntsman's chicken 92
   stuffed boiled chicken, 88
chicory: baked, 135
   salad and pear with Roquefort, 29
chocolate: chocolate cake, 153
   chocolate mousse, 150
   chocolate profiteroles, 152
   chocolate soufflé, 149
chou en salade, 39
citrus fruit, 12
civet de lièvre, 103
cod: cod steaks with quick-mustard sauce, 73
   pan-fried cod with mustard sauce, 72
   posh fish loaf, 85
   salt cod purée, 76

salt cod with garlic mayonnaise, 78
salt cod with potatoes, 77
colin poêlé petite sauce moutarde, 73
colin poêlé sauce moutarde, 72
compote d'abricots et de fraises, 140
concombres à la crème, 32
coq au vin, 90
coquilles Saint-Jacques à la crème et au safran, 66
coquilles Saint-Jacques au beurre blanc, 68
coquilles Saint-Jacques surprise, 69
côtes de porc au cidre et à l'oignon, 106
cottage pie, French, 119
crème anglaise, 140
crème fraîche, 12
crêpes farcies aux épinards, 41
croque-monsieur maison, 49
croûtes au fromage, 49
cucumber salad, creamy, 32
cumin, carrots cooked with, 125
custard, 140

daurade farcie aux amandes, 81
desserts, 136–55
Dublin Bay prawns, 61
duck: braised duck with turnips, 97
    duck breasts with orange, 95
    duck with olives, 96
    quick duck confit, 93
    roast duck with peaches, 96

eggs, 12
    eggs in red wine, 44
    eggs in the snow, 141
    floating island, 142
    gratin of eggs and Gruyère, 42
    hard-boiled eggs with anchovy mayonnaise, 36
    herb omelette, 45
    scrambled eggs PLM, 42
    scrambled eggs with *rillettes*, 43
    tomato and sweet pepper omelette, 46
emincé de carottes et de courgettes, 126
endives au four, 135
entrées chaudes, 40–59
escargots au Riesling, 48

faisan rôti farci, 98
family fish loaf, 84
feuilleté au Roquefort, 50
filets de merlan aux petits légumes, 79
fish and seafood, 60–85
    family fish loaf, 84
    fish stock, 12

Provençal fish soup, 71
see also individual types of fish
flageolet beans, simple, 129
flageolets au naturel, 129
floating island, 142
food processors, 12
French beans, 128
French cottage pie, 119
French pound cake, 155
fruit: vanilla and red fruit ice cream, 143

garlic mayonnaise, salt cod with, 78
garlic sauce, 109
gâteau à l'orange, 144
le gâteau au chocolat, 153
gâteau aux noix, 154
gâteau glacé au Moka, 145
gigot, 109
glace double à la vanille et aux fruits rouges, 143
gougère, 51
gratin d'aubergines, 127
gratin Dauphinois, 122
gratin de haddock au riz, 75
gratin of eggs and Gruyère, 42
gratin of smoked haddock, 75
gratinée au Roquefort, 21

hachis parmentier, 119
haddock: gratin of smoked haddock, 75
ham: ham in cream and port wine sauce, 59
    toasted cheese and ham, 49
hare, jugged, 103
haricot beans: improved canned haricot beans, 130
    pork and haricot bean casserole, 108
haricots en boîte améliorés, 130
haricots verts Fourchettes, 128
herbs, 12
herb omelette, 45
herb-stuffed tomatoes, 133
hollandaise, 12
hors d'oeuvre, 28 – 39
hot starters, 40 – 59
huntsman's chicken, 92
hygiene, 12

ice cream, vanilla and red fruit, 143
iced Mocha gâteau, 145
île flottante, 142
improved canned haricot beans, 130

jambon à la crème, 59
jugged hare, 103

kidneys in red wine, 113

lamb: lamb pot roast with onions and raisins,
112
lamb stew with turnips, 111
leg of lamb, 109
marinated lamb in foil, 110
langoustines, 61
lapin à la bière et aux pruneaux, 102
lapin à la moutarde, 101
lapin en daube, 100
lardons, 13
leeks: leek, carrot and potato soup, 22
leek salad, 30
leeks with cream, 124
lemon tart, 146
lentilles aux lardons, 134
lentils: lentil soup, 20
lentils with bacon, 134
lettuce: baby peas with lettuce and onions, 125
lotte à la Provençale, 74

macédoine de légumes frais à la mayonnaise, 38
magrets de canard à l'orange, 95
marinated lamb in foil, 110
mayonnaise, 13
celery root mayonnaise, 33
fresh vegetable medley with mayonnaise,
38
hard-boiled eggs with anchovy mayonnaise,
36
salt cod with garlic mayonnaise, 78
meat, 86–119
melons, chilled with sweet wine, 37
melons refraîchis au vin doux, 37
meringue: eggs in the snow, 141
meringue apples, 137
mixed vegetable tart, 56
monkfish with tomato and herbs, 74
moreu en aïoli, 78
morue parmentier, 77
moules farcies, 63
moules marinière, 62
mousse au chocolat, 150
mushrooms: creamy mushroom soup, 27
mushroom salad, 32
pan-fried mushrooms, 132
sautéed potatoes with mushrooms and bacon,
133
stuffed mushrooms, 130
trout with mushrooms, 80
veal in a cream and mushroom sauce, 104
veal with wild mushrooms, 105

mussels: mussel soup, 65
mussels in white wine, 62
mussels with potato salad, 64
stuffed mussels, 63
mustard: cod steaks with quick-mustard sauce,
73
mustard tart, 56
pan-fried cod with mustard sauce, 72
rabbit with mustard, 101

navarin d'agneau, 111

œufs à la neige, 141
œufs brouillés à la tourangelle, 43
œufs brouillés PLM, 42
œufs en meurette, 44
œufs gratinés, 42
œufs mimosa, 36
oil, 13
olives: black olive purée, 35
duck with olives, 96
omelette aux fines herbes, 45
onions: baby peas with lettuce and onions, 125
lamb pot roast with onions and raisins, 112
onion purée, 128
onion soup with Roquefort, 21
onion tart, 53
pan-fried pork chops with onion and vinegar,
106
Provençal onion and anchovy tart, 54
orange: orange cake, 144
duck breasts with, 95

pain de poisson de tous les jours, 84
pain de poisson pour invités, 85
pancakes stuffed with spinach, 41
partridges, pot-roasted, 94
peaches: peaches in white wine, 138
roast duck with peaches, 96
pears in red wine, 139
peas: baby peas with lettuce and onions, 125
fresh pea soup, 19
pêches au vin, 138
peeling, 13
peppercorns: steaks with pepper and anchovy, 118
peppers: Provençal hot-pepper sauce, 29
roasted pepper and tomato soup 24
sweet red pepper and avocado salad, 31
tomato and sweet pepper omelette, 46
perdreaux en casserole, 94
petit confit de canard, 93
petites bouchées, 52
petits pois à la laitue et aux petits oignons, 125

*petits soufflés fondants au chocolat au coulis de
  framboises*, 149
pheasant: pheasant terrine, 99
  stuffed roast pheasant, 98
pine nuts, trout with, 80
pipérade, 46
pissaladière, 54
pistachios: almond and pistachio charlotte, 151
pistou sauce, 18
poireaux à la crème, 124
poireaux vinaigrette, 30
poires au vin rouge, 139
pommes de terre à la forestière, 133
pommes de terre sautées Tata Boucher, 124
pommes meringuées, 137
porc à la boulangère, 107
pork: pan-fried pork chops with onion and
    vinegar, 106
  pork and haricot bean casserole, 108
  roast pork with potatoes, 107
posh fish loaf, 85
pot au feu, 116
potage à l'oseille, 22
potage au potiron, 17
potage bonne femme, 22
potage Saint-Germain, 19
potatoes: creamed potatoes, 123
  leek, carrot and potato soup, 22
  mussels with potato salad, 64
  potato gratin, 122
  roast pork with potatoes, 107
  salt cod with potatoes, 77
  sautéed potatoes, 124
  sautéed potatoes with mushrooms and bacon,
    133
poularde à la Tourangelle, 91
la poule au pot farcie, 88
poulet au vinaigre, 89
poulet chasseur, 92
poultry and game, 86–103
pound cake, French 155
profiteroles au chocolat, 152
Provençal fish soup, 71
Provençal hot-pepper sauce, 29
Provençal onion and anchovy tart, 54
prunes: rabbit with ale and prunes, 102
pumpkin soup, 17
purée de pommes de terre Marthe, 123
purée d'oignons, 128

quatre-quarts, 155
quiche lorraine, 55
quick duck confit, 93

rabbit: pot-roasted rabbit, 100
  rabbit with ale and prunes, 102
  rabbit with mustard, 101
ragout of Provençal vegetables, 121
raie au beurre noir, 73
raisins: lamb pot roast with onions and raisins,
  112
ratatouille, 121
rice: gratin of smoked haddock, 75
rillettes de saumon, 36
  scrambled eggs with, 43
roast salmon with saffron sauce, 70
rognons au vin rouge, 113
Roquefort cheese puff, 50
rouille, 29

saffron cream, scallops with, 66
salad spinner, 13
salade d'endive et de poire au Roquefort, 29
salade de moules aux pommes de terre, 64
salade de poivrons à l'avocat, 31
salade de tomates, 34
salads: creamy cucumber, 32
  grated carrot, 39
  leek, 30
  mushroom, 32
  shredded cabbage, 39
  sweet red pepper and avocado, 31
  tomato, 34
salmon: roast salmon with saffron sauce, 70
  salmon rillettes, 36
  sole and salmon terrine, 83
salt cod: *see* cod
sauces: hollandaise, 12
  pistou, 18
  Provençal hot-pepper, 29
  raspberry sauce, 149
  sauce à l'ail, 109
  sauce blanche, 13
saumon cuit au four avec une petite sauce safranée, 70
savoury puffs, 52
scallops: scallops with a puff pastry lid, 69
  scallops with saffron cream, 66
  scallops with shallot butter, 68
scampi, 61
scissors, 15
sea bream with almond stuffing, 81
sea salt, 15
seafood and fish, 60–85
shallot butter, scallops with, 68
skate in black butter, 73
snails with wine sauce, 48
sole and salmon terrine, 83

sorrel soup, 22
soufflé au Gruyère, 47
soupe au pistou, 18
soupe au poivron et à la tomate, 24
soupe aux lentilles, 20
soupe de moules, 65
soupe de poissons Madame Bastier, 71
soupe fraîche aux épinards et à l'avocat, 26
soups, 16–27
    chilled spinach and avocado, 26
    creamy mushroom, 27
    fresh pea, 19
    leek, carrot and potato, 22
    lentil, 20
    mussel, 65
    onion soup with Roquefort, 21
    Provençal fish, 71
    pumpkin, 17
    roast pepper and tomato, 24
    sorrel, 22
    vegetable soup with basil, garlic and cheese, 18
spatulas, 15
spinach: chilled spinach and avocado soup, 26
    pancakes stuffed with spinach, 41
    spinach tart, 57
steaks au poivre et aux anchois, 118
stock: chicken, 12
    fish, 12
strawberry and apricot compote, 140

tagine de mouton Yonnée, 112
tapenade, 35
tarte à la moutarde, 56
tarte à l'oignon, 53
tarte à la ratatouille, 56
tarte au citron, 146
tarte aux épinards, 57
tarte Tatin, 148
tarte aux tomates toute simple, 58
tarts: caramelised upside-down apple tart, 148
    lemon tart, 146
    mixed vegetable tart, 56
    mustard tart, 56
    onion tart, 53
    Provençal onion and anchovy tart, 54
    quick upside-down apple tart, 147
    spinach tart, 57
    tomato tart, 58

Tatin express, 147
terrine de faisan, 99
terrine de poissons Anne-Sophie, 83
timing, 15
tomates farcies bijou, 133
tomatoes: herb-stuffed tomatoes, 133
    monkfish with tomato and herbs, 74
    roasted pepper and tomato soup, 24
    tomato and sweet pepper omelette, 46
    tomato *coulis*, 15
    tomato salad, 34
    tomato tart, 58
trout: trout with mushrooms, 80
    trout with pine nuts, 80
    truite aux champignons, 80
    truite aux pignons, 80
turnips: braised duck with turnips, 97
    lamb stew with turnips, 111

vanilla and red fruit ice cream, 143
veal: veal in a cream and mushroom sauce, 104
    veal with wild mushrooms, 105
    veaux au girolles, 105
vegetables, 120–35
    fresh vegetable medley with mayonnaise, 38
    mixed vegetable tart, 56
    ragout of Provençal vegetables, 121
    vegetable soup with basil, garlic and cheese, 18
velouté aux champignons, 27
vichyssoise aux asperges et fines herbes, 25
vinaigrette, 15
vinegar: chicken with a vinegar sauce, 89
    pan-fried pork chops with onion and vinegar, 106

walnut cake, 154
white sauce, 13
whiting: baked whiting fillets with vegetables, 79
wine: beef cooked in red Burgundy, 114
    chicken cooked in red wine, 90
    chicken cooked in a wine and cream sauce, 91
    chilled melons with sweet wine, 37
    eggs in red wine, 44
    kidneys in red wine, 113
    mussels in white wine, 62
    peaches in white wine, 138
    pears in red wine, 139
    snails with wine sauce, 48